HACKING EXPOSED

by
Soumya Ranjan Behera

BPB PUBLICATIONS

Distributors:

BPB PUBLICATIONS 20,
Ansari Road, Darya Ganj
New Delhi-110002
Ph: 23254990/23254991

BPB BOOK CENTRE
376 Old Lajpat Rai Market,
Delhi-110006
Ph: 23861747

COMPUTER BOOK CENTRE
12, Shrungar Shopping Centre,
M.G.Road, BENGALURU–560001
Ph: 25587923/25584641

DECCAN AGENCIES
4-3-329, Bank Street,
Hyderabad-500195
Ph: 24756967/24756400

MICRO MEDIA
Shop No. 5, Mahendra Chambers, 150 DN
Rd. Next to Capital Cinema, V.T. (C.S.T.)
Station, MUMBAI-400 001
Ph: 22078296/22078297

Published by Manish Jain for BPB Publications, 20, Ansari Road, Darya Ganj, New Delhi-110002 and Printed by Repro India Pvt Ltd, Mumbai

DISCLAIMER

This book has been published for education purpose only. Readers are advised to examine the privacy policy, organization policies and the laws of respective countries before taking their own decisions. The publisher and author are not liable for any steps that a reader may take based on this publication and are not responsible for any steps that may have been taken after reading the publication. Microsoft Windows and any other marks used (Pictures, Screen Shots, etc.) have been used descriptively as the marks are owned by third parties.

PREFACE

Hacking is the art of creative problem solving, whether that means finding an unconventional solution to a difficult problem or exploiting holes in sloppy programming. Many people call themselves hackers, but few have the strong technical foundation needed to really push the envelope. Rather than merely showing how to run existing exploits, author **Soumya Ranjan Behera** explains how hacking techniques actually work. To share the art and science of hacking in a way that is accessible to everyone, **Hacking Exposed** introduces practical hacking techniques from a hacker's perspective.

Hackers are always pushing the boundaries, investigating the unknown, and evolving their art. This book will give you a complete picture network communications, and existing hacking techniques. Combine this knowledge with the accompanying Linux environment, and all you need is your own creativity.

DEDICATED TO

People's president and Missile man
Late Dr. A. P. J. Abdul Kalam

"You have to dream before your dreams can come true."

Table of Contents

Chapter – 4 : Hacking Skills and Tools

Chapter – 8 : Scanning

Chapter – 9 : Cryptography

Chapter – 10 : Steganography

Chapter – 13 : Sniffing, Packet Analyzer and Session Hijacking

Chapter – 14 : Denial of Service (DoS) Attack

Chapter – 15 : Wireless Network Hacking

Chapter – 16 : Web Server & Application Vulnerabilities

Chapter – 17 : Penetration Testing

CHAPTER 1

Introduction to Hacking

Hacking

"Hacking is exploiting security controls either in a technical, physical or a human-based element."

– Kevin Mitnick

Gaining unauthorized access to data in a system or computer is hacking. However, the word *hacking* has two definitions. The first definition refers to the hobby/profession of working with computers. The second definition refers to modifies computer hardware or software in a way that changes the creator's original intent.

It is also defined as the art of exploiting computers to get access to otherwise unauthorized information. Now that the world is using IT systems to gather, store, and manipulate important information; there is also a need to make sure that data is secure. However, no system is without is problems. Holes are often present within security systems, which, if exploited, allow hackers to gain access to this otherwise restricted information.

> **NOTE** A *hacker* is a person who finds and exploits the fault in computer systems and networks to gain access. They are usually expert in computer programing and computer security.

Ethical Hacking

It refers to the act of locating weaknesses and vulnerabilities of computer and information systems by duplicating the intent and actions of malicious hackers. It is also known as penetration testing, intrusion testing, or red teaming.

> **NOTE** An ethical hacker is a security professional who applies their hacking skills for defensive purposes on behalf of the owners of information systems. Ethical hackers are also known as *white hat hackers*.

Importance of ethical hacking

In today's digital era, the biggest threats to any business organization and government organization come from cyber criminals. Nowadays, as more and more companies are entering the e-commerce ecosystem and adopting new technologies, like cloud computing, the threat from imminent security breaches is clearly demanding the need for efficient information security systems.

Hacking can lead to loss of business for organizations that deal in finance. Ethical hacking puts them a step ahead of the cyber criminals who would otherwise lead to loss of business.

> **NOTE** Ethical hacking includes services like application testing, remote or war dialing, local network testing, wireless security, system hardening, social engineering, etc.

Hacker

Hackers have been around for so many years. Since the computer and Internet became widely used in the world, we have started to hear more and more about hacking.

As the term *hacking* has two meanings, so does the term *hacker* is a word that has two meanings:

Traditionally, a *hacker* is someone who likes to play with software or electronic systems. They enjoy exploring and learning how computer systems operate.

Recently, a *hacker* has taken on a new meaning that someone who finds weaknesses in a computer and computer network, though the term can also refer to someone with an advanced understanding of computers and computer networks.

Normally, hackers are people who try to gain unauthorized access to your computer.

Hacker classification

Hackers are classified according to their motive and type of work. *The following list helps you to better understand the types of hackers.*

White hat hacker

A *white hat hacker* is computer security expert who specializes in penetration testing and in other testing methodologies to ensure the security of an organization's information systems. They are also known as *ethical hacker*. Generally, white hat hackers are the good guys in the world of hackers.

 NOTE *Ethical hacking* is a term coined by IBM meant to imply a broader category than just penetration testing.

Black hat hacker

A *black hat hacker* is an individual with extensive computer knowledge whose purpose is to breach or bypass Internet security. They are also known as *crackers* or *dark-side hackers*. They are computer security hackers who break into computers and networks or also create computer viruses. Generally, ethical hackers build things and crackers break things.

Gray hat hacker

A *gray hat hacker* is a combination of a black hat and a white hat hacker. It may relate to whether they sometimes arguably act illegally, though in good will, or to show how they disclose vulnerabilities. They usually do not hack for personal gain or have malicious intentions, but may be prepared to technically commit crimes during the course of their technological exploits in order to achieve better security.

Script kiddie

A *script kiddie* (or *skiddie*) is a non-expert who uses existing scripts, code, or other tools illegally to gain entry to a computer system or network, without understanding the way the tools function or the way the system or network is designed. Although they may have some programming skill, script kiddies do not have the experience to write their own programs that exploit vulnerabilities.

Hacktivist

A *hacktivist* is a hacker who utilizes technology to announce a social, ideological, religious, or political message. Most of the hacktivism involves website defacement or denial-of-service attacks.

Phases of hacking

The process of hacking can be broken down into five distinct phases, which are described as follows:

Phase 1 – Reconnaissance
Phase 2 – Scanning
Phase 3 – Gaining access
Phase 4 – Maintaining access
Phase 5 – Covering tracks

Reconnaissance

Reconnaissance is the primary phase where the hacker gathers information about a target using active or passive means.

Passive reconnaissance involves gathering information regarding a potential target without the target's knowledge. It is usually done by using Internet searches of an individual or company to gain information. This process is generally called *information gathering*.

Sniffing the network is a type of passive reconnaissance and can produce useful information, such as IP address ranges, naming conventions, hidden servers or networks, and other available services on the system or network. Sniffing network traffic is similar to building monitoring: a hacker watches the flow of data to see what time certain transactions take place and where the traffic is going.

Active reconnaissance involves penetrating the network to discover individual hosts, IP addresses, and services on the network. It generally involves more risk of detection than passive reconnaissance. It is also called *rattling the doorknobs*.

 NOTE Some widely used reconnaissance tools are NMAP, Hping, Maltego, and Google Dorks.

Scanning

In *scanning*, the information gathered during the reconnaissance phase is used to scan the perimeter and internal network devices looking for weaknesses. It includes scanning the target for services running, open ports, firewall detection, finding vulnerabilities, OS detection, etc.

Tools that a hacker may use during the scanning phase include dialers, port scanners, network mappers, vulnerability scanners, Internet Control Message Protocol (ICMP) scanners, ping sweeps, and Simple Network Management Protocol (SNMP) sweepers.

Hackers are looking for any information that can help them perpetrate an attack on a target, such as computer names, operating system (OS), user accounts, IP addresses, and installed software.

 NOTE Some widely used scanning tools are Nessus, Nexpose, and NMAP.

Gaining access

After scanning, a hacker strategies the blueprint of the network of the target with the help of data collected during Phase 1 (Reconnaissance) and Phase 2 (Scanning). In this phase, the hacker would exploit a vulnerability to gain access to the target. It generally involves taking control of one or more network devices to extract data from the target or use that device to perform attacks on other targets.

Hackers perform certain types of hacking attacks, such as stack-based buffer overflows, denial-of-service (DoS), and session hijacking. This hacking attack can be delivered to the target system via a local area network (LAN), either wired or wireless; local access to a PC; the Internet (online); or offline. Gaining access is known in the hacker world as *owning* the system. Because, once a system has been hacked, the hacker has all the controls of the system and can run that system according to them.

NOTE   The primary tool that is used in this process is Metasploit.

Maintaining access

After gaining access, the hacker wants to keep that access for future exploitation and attacks to collect more data. Sometimes, hackers create a harder security for the system by using backdoors, rootkits, and Trojans so that no other hackers or security personnel can breach it.

NOTE   *Zombie system* is a computer connected to the Internet that has been compromised by a hacker, computer virus, or Trojan horse program and can be used to perform malicious tasks of one sort or another under remote direction.

Covering tracks

In the final phase, hackers cover their tracks to avoid detection by security personnel. To avoid legal action on them, hackers remove evidence of hacking, such as deletion or alteration of log files, exfiltration of data via DNS tunneling or steganography, clearing out sent e-mails, and clearing temp files.

Types of hacking attacks

There are several ways in which hackers can target and attack the devices and networks. So, some of the most common hacking techniques are listed as follows:

- **Social engineering:** This is a form of techniques engaged by cybercriminals designed to trap normal and common users into sending their confidential data, infecting their computers with malware, or opening links to infected sites.

- **Malware attack**: This is specifically designed by cybercriminals to gain access or damage a computer without the knowledge of the owner by injecting malicious software through Internet or by other storage devices.

- **Password cracking:** This is meant to gain unauthorized access to a computer without the computer owner's awareness by decoding the password.

- **Phishing:** This involves one program, system, or website successfully masquerading as another by gaining confidential information, such as user IDs, passwords, bank details, and thereby being treated as a trusted system by a user or another program.

- **Session hijacking:** This is a method of taking over a Web user session by stealthily obtaining the session ID and masquerading as the authorized user. It is also known as *cookie hijacking*.

- **DoS (denial-of-service) attack:** This is aimed to bring the network to its knees by flooding it with useless traffic, such as invalid authentication requests, which eventually brings the whole network down.

- **Web hacking:** This is any attack that attempts to breach a website. *SQL injection* and *cross-site scripting* are the common hacking types of web hacking.

Essential terminologies

Backdoor is a hidden entry to a computing device or software that bypasses security measures, such as logins and password protections.

Bot is a computer that has been compromised with malware attack and can be controlled remotely by a hacker. A hacker can then use the bot (also known as a zombie computer) to launch more attacks, or to bring it into a collection of controlled computers, known as a *botnet*.

Bug is a flaw or error in a software program.

Cracking is defined by breaking into a security system, usually for nefarious purposes.

Exploit is a way or process to take advantage of a bug or vulnerability in a computer or application.

Phreak is someone who breaks into the telephone network illegally, to make free calls or to tap phone lines.

Vulnerability is a weakness that allows a hacker to compromise the security of a computer or network system.

CHAPTER 2

Cybercrime and Security

Cybercrime

Any unlawful acts that involve a computer and a network is defined as cybercrime.

Types of cybercrime

Cybercrime can be classified into four major categories.

Cybercrime against person

- *Cyber stalking* means unwanted or obsessive attention by an individual or group toward another person through the use of computer technology such as the Internet, e-mails, SMS, webcams, phones calls, websites, or even videos.

- *Hacking* is gaining unauthorized access over a computer system with the intent of personal gain or misuse.

- *Cracking* means digitally removing the copyright protection code of a computer program or software.

- *Defamation* is the technique of damaging the reputation of someone using a computer or electronic service and the Internet.

- *Identity theft* occurs when someone steals your identity and pretends to be you to access resources such as credit cards, bank accounts, and other benefits in your name.

- *Online fraud* is act of stealing confidential details (such as bank details, personal details, card details) of a victim using phishing and spamming for gaining or withdrawing money from the victim's account.

- *Child pornography* involves the use of electronic device and services to create, distribute, or access materials that sexually exploit minor children.

- *Spoofing* means imitate something while exaggerating its characteristic features with some personal gain or profit.

Cybercrime against property

- *Transferring virus* into someone's computer programs, disk drive, files, or booting sector of hard drive using an e-mail attachment as a medium to slowing down or destroy the system.

- *Cybersquatting* refers to two or more persons claiming for the same or approximately identical domain name or any service available on the Internet (such as a profile of Facebook, Twitter, Instagram).

- *Cyber vandalism* means destroying or damaging the data during the unavailability of a network service.

- *Intellectual property crime* is any illegal act by which the owner is deprived of his/her rights completely or partially. These crimes deal with copyrights, trademark, software piracy, infringement of patents, designs, source code, etc.

Cybercrime against government

- *Cyber warfare* is an online conflict that involves politically motivated attacks on information and its related systems by hijacking or disabling the official websites, disrupting the network connection, stealing or altering the classified information of government or financial institutions.

- *Cyber terrorism* is also an Internet-based attack that includes large-scale attacks to create a havoc on computer networks using malware or viruses, to attack governments and organizations.

Cybercrime against society

- *Online gambling* is defined as gaining money through gambling over the Internet. It is also known as Internet gambling or iGambling.

- *Cyber trafficking* is defined as any illegal trading over the Internet using computer and/or computer services.

Cyber-attack and its sources

A cyber-attack is defined as a malicious attempt to damage or disrupt a computer network or system. Virus attacks hamper important work involved with data and documents. That's why it is the most powerful and vulnerable threat to computer users. It is vital for every computer user to be aware about the software and programs that

can help to protect the personal computers from attacks. The major sources of cyber-attacks are highlighted as follows.

Downloadable programs

Downloadable programs and files are one of the best possible sources of virus attack. Any executable program and file are the major sources. If a user want to download a programs or file from the Internet, then user needs to scan it before downloading.

Pirated or cracked software

Pirated or cracked software are illegal to download. Most people who download them from online sources are unaware that they may contain viruses and bug sources as well. These types of viruses and bugs are difficult to detect and remove. So, a user should always download original software from the appropriate source.

Email attachments

Anyone can send you an e-mail attachment whether you know them or not. Clicking on unknown links or attachments can harm your computer. It is necessary to scan the e-mail attachment before downloading.

Internet

One of the easiest ways to get a virus in your device is through the Internet. Make sure to check the URL before accessing any website. For a secured URL, always look for *https* in it.

Booting from an unknown CD

A malicious software can get into your device through an unknown CD. A good practice to be safe from malicious infection is to remove the CD when your device is not working at all. Your system could reboot the CD if it is not removed before switching off the computer.

Infected flash drives or disks

Flash drives and disks are the main cause of spreading viruses. A virus can also be copied from one computer to other when the user copies infected files using flash drives and disks. To prevent it, a user must scan it before transferring any files from an unknown user.

Symptoms of malware attack

While these types of malware differ greatly in how they spread and infect computers, they all can produce similar symptoms. Computers that are infected with malware can exhibit any of the following symptoms:

- Increased CPU usage.
- Slow computer or web browser speedProblems connecting to networks.
- Freezing or crashing.
- Modified or deleted files.
- Appearance of strange files, programs, or desktop icons.
- Programs running, turning off, or reconfiguring themselves (malware will often reconfigure or turn off antivirus and firewall programs).
- Strange computer behavior.
- E-mails/messages being sent automatically and without the user's knowledge (a friend receives a strange e-mail from you that you did not send).

Cyber security

The security applied to computers, as well as computer networks such as private and public networks, including the Internet is called as *cyber security* or *IT security*. Cybersecurity is the process of applying security measures to ensure confidentiality, integrity, and availability of data.

Computer protection (countermeasures)

Computer protection is an action, device, procedure, or technique that reduces a threat, vulnerability, or an attack by eliminating or preventing it.

Methods to provide protection

Some primary methods to provide protection are as follows:

- *System access control* is a method that does not allow any unauthorized access of a system.

- *Data access control* is a method in which a user can monitor who can access what data and for what purpose. A user can set the rules for based-on-security level of other user.

- *System and security administration* monitors and allocates system resources such as disk space, performs backups, provides user access, manages user accounts and system security functions.

- *Secure by design* means that the hardware and software have been designed from the ground up to be secure.

Components of computer security

The basic components of a computer security system are as follows:

- *Confidentiality* is the process of keeping data and information secret and hidden from threats.

- *Integrity* is the process protecting data and information from being modified by unknown and unauthorized parties.

- *Availability* of information refers to ensuring that authorized parties are able to access the information when needed.

- *Access control* ensures that only authorized users can access resources.

- *Authentication* is a process that ensures and confirms a user's identity.

- *Non-repudiation* means to ensure that a transferred message has been sent and received by the parties claiming to have sent and received the message.

- *Privacy* ensures that information is available only to those who have the right to use it.

- *Steganography* is the technique of hiding confidential information within any media. It can be applied to images, video files, or audio files. It helps to maintain confidentiality and integrity of data.

- *Cryptography* is a technique to provide message confidentiality. In Greek, it means *secret writing*. It involves the process of encryption and decryption.

  Some commonly used terms related to cryptography are as follows:

  - *Plaintext* is the original message or data that as input.
  - *Encryption* is the process of changing plaintext into cipher text using an encryption algorithm.
  - *Cipher text* is the encrypted form of the message. It is the scrambled message produced as an output.
  - *Decryption* is the process of changing cipher text into plain text using a decryption algorithm.
  - *Key* also acts as input to the encryption algorithm. The exact substitutions and transformations performed by the algorithm depend on the key. Thus, a key is a number or a set of numbers that the algorithm uses to perform encryption and decryption.

Solution to computer security threats

Some major solutions to prevent and protect computer security threats are described as follows.

Antivirus software

Antivirus programs are installed onto your computer and can scan and remove known viruses that you may have contracted. The software can also be set to automatically scan diskettes when inserted into the disk drive, scan files when downloaded from the Internet, or scan e-mail when received.

Antivirus or anti-virus software are used to prevent, detect, and remove malware, including but not limited to computer viruses, computer worms, Trojan horses, spyware, and adware. Computer security, including protection from social engineering techniques, is commonly offered in products and services of antivirus software companies.

Some major antivirus software are: Quick-Heal, AVG, Kaspersky, Avira, Bit-defender, McAfee, Trend Micro, K7, and Norton.

Digital certificate

Digital certificate is an electronic *passport* that allows a person, computer, or organization to exchange information securely over the Internet using the Public Key Infrastructure (PKI). It is also referred as a Public Key Certificate.

Digital signature

Digital signature is an electronic form of signature that is used to validate the authenticity and integrity of a message, software, or digital document. It is also known as an electronic signature. It is generally used in e-commerce, software distribution, financial transactions, and other situations that rely on forgery or tampering detection techniques.

Firewall

It protects private networks by securing gateway servers to external networks such as the Internet. It guards any network against hacks, cyber-attacks, and other unauthorized user access. It can be a standalone machine or software in a router or server. Thus, it is classified into two type: hardware firewall and software firewall. Advanced firewalls operate on the application layer of a network stack. This means they are capable of intercepting all packets traveling to or from running software. Application firewalls apply their filtering rules per process (i.e., to allow or block), instead of filtering connections by port.

Password

A password is a sequence of characters used to verify the identity of a user during the authentication process. It is mostly used in conjunction with a username or user ID. It is designed to be known only to the user and allow that user to gain access to a device, application, or website. When a password is entered, the computer system hides the password field with asterisks or bullets for security purposes.

Generally, there are two modes of password as follows:

- **Weak password:** This is short and consists solely of letters or numbers. It is very easy to remember, such as the name, phone number, birthdate. It is easy to crack.

- **Strong password:** This is a combination of alphabets (both upper- and lowercase), numbers, and special characteristics. It is difficult to crack.

File and folder access permissions

File and folder access permissions is a method to assign permissions or access rights to specific users and groups of users to view, change, navigate, and execute the contents of the files and folders.

Some specific permissions are as follows:

- **Read:** Permits viewing or accessing of the file's and folder's contents.

- **Write:** Permits writing and adding of files and folder.

- **Read and Execute:** Permits viewing and accessing of the file's contents, as well as executing of the file.

- **Modify:** Permits reading and writing of the file; allows deletion of the file or folder.

- **Full control:** Permits reading, writing, changing, and deleting of files and folders.

Laws relating to cybercrime in India

To deal with growing cybercrime in India, the Government of India (GoI) has imposed the Information Technology Act, 2000, which was enacted with the prime objective to create an enabling environment for commercial use of **information technology (IT)**. *Some major acts and laws are described below:*

Cybercrimes under the IT Act

- Section 65: Tampering with computer source documents.
- Section 66: Hacking with computer systems, data alteration.
- Section 66B: Receiving stolen computer or communication device.
- Section 66C: Using password of another person.
- Section 66D: Cheating by personation by using a computer resource.
- Section 66E: Violation of privacy (publishing private images of others).
- Section 66F: Acts of cyber terrorism.
- Section 67: Publishing obscene information in electronic form.
- Section 67A: Publishing or transmitting of material containing sexually explicit act, etc. in electronic form.
- Section 67B: Publishing child porn or predating children online.
- Section 67C: Intermediary intentionally or knowingly contravening the directions about preservation and retention of information.
- Section 68: Failure/refusal to comply with orders.
- Section 69: Failure/refusal to decrypt data/information.
- Section 70: Unauthorized access to protected systems.
- Section 71: Penalty for misrepresentation.
- Section 72: Breach of confidentiality and privacy.
- Section 72A: Disclosure of information in breach of lawful contract.
- Section 73: Publishing false digital signature or certificates.
- Section 74: Publication for fraudulent purposes.

Cybercrimes under IPC and special laws

- Section 503 IPC: Sending threatening messages by e-mails.
- Section 499 IPC: Sending defamatory messages by e-mails.
- Section 463 IPC: Forgery of electronic records.
- Section 420 IPC: Fake websites, cyber frauds.

- Section 463 IPC: E-mail spoofing.
- Section 383 IPC: Web-jacking.
- Section 500 IPC: Sending abusive message by e-mails.

Cybercrimes under the special acts

- NDPS (Narcotic Drugs and Psychotropic Substances) Act: Online sale of drugs.
- Arms act: Online sales of arms and ammunitions.

CHAPTER 3

Computer Network System and DNS Working

Computer network

A computer network is defined as the interconnection of two or more computers. It is done to enable the computers to communicate and share available resources.

Applications of a computer network

- Sharing of resources, such as printers.
- Sharing of expensive software and database.
- Communication from one computer to another computer.
- Exchange of data and information among users via network.
- Sharing of information over geographically wide areas.

Types of computer networks

Some major types of computer networks are as follows.

Local area network

A **local area network** (**LAN**) is designed for small physical areas such as an office, group of buildings, or a factory. LANs are used widely as they are easy to design and to troubleshoot. Personal computers and workstations are connected to each other through LANs. We can use different types of topologies through LAN, including Star, Ring, Bus, Tree, etc. A LAN can be a simple network such as connecting two computers, to share files and network among each other, while it can also be as complex as interconnecting an entire building. LANs are also widely used to share resources such as printers, shared hard drives, etc.

Metropolitan area network

A **metropolitan area network** (**MAN**) is basically a bigger version of LAN. It uses the similar technology as LAN. It covers a large geographical area and may serve as an **ISP** (**Internet service provider**). A MAN is designed for customers who need a high-speed connectivity. The data transfer rate and the propagation delay of MAN are moderate. Devices used for transmission of data through MAN are: modem and wire/cable. Examples of a MAN are the part of the telephone company network that can provide a high-speed DSL line to the customer or the cable TV network in a city.

Wide area network

A **wide area network** (**WAN**) is a computer network that extends over a large geographical area, although it might be confined within the bounds of a state or country. A WAN could be a connection of LAN connecting to other LANs via telephone lines and radio waves and may be limited to an enterprise (a corporation or an organization) or accessible to the public. The technology is high speed and relatively expensive. Devices used for transmission of data through WAN are optic wires, microwaves, and satellites. There are two types of WAN: switched WAN and point-to-point WAN. Example of a switched WAN is the **asynchronous transfer mode** (**ATM**) network, and example of a point-to-point WAN is a dial-up line that connects a home computer to the Internet.

Personal area network

A **personal area network** (**PAN**) is the smallest type of network, which is made up of a wireless modem, a computer or two, phones, printers, tablets, etc., and revolves around one person in one building. These types of networks are typically found in small offices or residences and are managed by one person or organization from a single device.

Virtual private network

A **virtual private network** (**VPN**) is a technology that creates a safe and encrypted connection over a less secure network, such as the Internet. VPN technology was developed as a way to allow remote users and branch offices to securely access corporate applications and other resources. To ensure safety, data travels through secure tunnels, and VPN users must use authentication methods including passwords, tokens, and other unique identification methods to gain access to the VPN.

> NOTE
>
> *Server* is a device that is shared by several users of a network.
>
> *File server* is a computer on a network that is used to provide users on a network with access to files.

Internet connections

An Internet connection is a service that provides access to the global system of interconnected computer networks. The speed of the Internet connection depends on the bandwidth.

Types of Internet connections

Some major types of Internet connections are described as follows.

Dial-up connection

A dial-up connection technology dials into the network through an existing phone line, creating a semi-permanent link to the Internet. Operating on a single channel, it monopolizes the phone line and is the slowest method of accessing the Internet. It is often the only form of Internet access available in rural areas, as it requires no infrastructure, other than the already existing telephone network, to connect to the Internet. Usually, dial-up connections do not exceed a speed of 56 kbit/s, as they are primarily made via a 56k modem.

Broadband connection

The term *broadband connection* includes a broad range of technologies, all of which provide high data rate access to the Internet. It provides a continuous connection; there is no dial-up/in process required and it does not "hog" phone lines. It truly is the most used form of Internet access because of its high access speeds. A broadband connection is offered in different forms as follows:

- **Digital subscriber line (DSL)**: This uses an existing two-wire copper telephone line connected to the premise, so service is delivered simultaneously with wired telephone service; it will not tie up your phone line as an analog dial-up connection does. The two main categories of DSL for home subscribers are called ADSL and SDSL. All types of DSL technologies are collectively referred to as xDSL. An xDSL connection's speed ranges from 128 Kbps to 9 Mbps.

- **Cable modem**: This transmits data via airwaves on the cable television infrastructure. It is provided by the local cable TV provider through a cable modem. Data is transmitted via a coaxial cable or a hybrid fiber coaxial cable. Cable speeds range from 512 Kbps to 20 Mbps.

- **Fiber optic**: This transfers data fully or partially via fiber optic cables. "Fiber" refers to the thin glass wires inside the larger protective cable. "Optic" refers to the way the type of data transferred light signals. Fiber connections can provide homes and businesses with data transfer speeds of 1 Gbps.

- **Broadband over power line (BPL)**: This technology makes possible high-speed Internet and home network access over ordinary residential electrical lines and power cables. It was created as an alternative to other wired broadband Internet systems such as the DSL and cable modem. Some people use the term BPL to refer specifically to the home networking aspects of power line communications and **IPL** (Internet over power line) to refer to long-distance Internet usages.

Wireless connection

In a wireless type of Internet connection, radio frequency bands are used in place of telephone or cable networks. This Internet connection is the "always-on" connection that can be accessed from any location that falls within the network coverage. Wireless connections are made possible through the use of a modem, which picks up Internet signals and sends them to other devices. Some ways to connect the Internet wirelessly are as follows:

- **Wireless fidelity (Wi-Fi)**: Wi-Fi uses radio waves to provide wireless high-speed Internet and network connections. Wireless (or Wi-Fi) hotspots are essentially wireless access points providing network and/or Internet access to mobile devices such as your laptop or smartphone, typically in public locations, such as shopping malls, restaurants, hotels, airports, railway station, parks, etc.

- **Worldwide Interoperability for Microwave Access (WiMAX)**: This is a standardized wireless version of Ethernet intended primarily as an alternative to wire technologies (such as cable modems, DSL) to provide broadband access to customer premises. It would operate similar to Wi-Fi, but at higher speeds over greater distances and for a greater number of users.

- **Mobile wireless broadband service**: This is also called as mobile broadband. It also referred to as WWAN (for wireless wide area network) and is a general term used to describe high-speed Internet access from mobile providers for portable devices. Mobile broadband services can also provide wireless Internet access on your laptop or netbook using built-in mobile broadband network cards or other portable network devices, such as USB modems or portable Wi-Fi mobile hotspots.

- **Internet over satellite (IoS)**: IoS allows a user to access the Internet via a satellite that orbits the earth. A satellite is placed at a static point above the earth's surface, in a fixed position. The enormous distance that a signal travels from the earth to the satellite and back again provides a delayed connection compared to cable and DSL.

Intranet is a private network, operated by a large company or other organization, which uses Internet technologies, but is insulated from the global Internet.

Extranet is an intranet that is accessible to some people from outside the company, or possibly shared by more than one organization.

Integrated Services Digital Network (ISDN) is a telecommunications technology that enables the transmission of digital data over standard phone lines. It can be used for voice calls, as well as data transfers. It supports data transfer rates of 64 Kbps.

Network architecture

Network architectures can be broadly classified as using either peer-to-peer or client/server architecture.

Peer-to-peer network

A peer-to-peer network is also known as a P2P network. In this, each workstation has equivalent capabilities and responsibilities. This differs from the client/server architecture in which some workstations are dedicated to serving the others. Peer-to-peer networks are generally simpler and less expensive, but they usually do not offer the same performance under heavy loads.

Client/Server network

In a client/server architecture, each computer or process on the network is either a client or a server. Servers are powerful computers or processors dedicated to managing disk drives (file servers), printers (print servers), or network traffic (network servers). Clients are less powerful PC workstations on which users run applications. Clients rely on servers for resources, such as files, devices, and even processing power.

OSI model

There are so many users who use a computer network and are located over the world. So, the International organization of Standardization (ISO) has developed a standard to ensure, national and worldwide data communication, systems must be developed that are compatible to communicate with each other. This is called a model for Open System Interconnection (OSI) and is commonly known as the OSI model.

This model has a seven-layer architecture. It defines seven layers or levels in a complete communication system.

- **Application**: The application layer is the layer that the users and user applications most often interact with. Network communication is discussed in terms of availability of resources, partners to communicate with, and data synchronization.

- **Presentation**: The presentation layer is responsible for mapping resources and creating context. It is used to translate lower-level networking data into data that applications expect to see.

- **Session**: The session layer is a connection handler. It creates, maintains, and destroys connections between nodes in a persistent way.

- **Transport**: The transport layer is responsible for handing the layers above it a reliable connection. In this context, reliable refers to the ability to verify that a piece of data was received intact at the other end of the connection. This layer can resend information that has been dropped or corrupted and can acknowledge the receipt of data to remote computers.

- **Network**: The network layer is used to route data between different nodes on the network. It uses addresses to be able to identify which computer to send information to. This layer can also breakdown larger messages into smaller chunks to be reassembled on the opposite end.

- **Data link**: This layer is implemented as a method of establishing and maintaining reliable links between different nodes or devices on a network using existing physical connections.

- **Physical**: The physical layer is responsible for handling the actual physical devices that are used to make a connection. This layer involves the bare software that manages physical connections as well as the hardware itself (like Ethernet).

Network devices

Network devices are components used to connect computers or other electronic devices together so that they can share files or resources. Different networking devices have different roles to play in a computer network. Some major computer networking devices are as follows.

Repeater

A repeater operates at the physical layer. Its job is to regenerate the signal over the same network before the signal becomes too weak or corrupted so as to extend the length to which the signal can be transmitted over the same network. An important point to be noted about repeaters is that they do no amplify the signal. When the signal becomes weak, they copy the signal bit-by-bit and regenerate it at the original strength. It is a two-port device.

Hub

A hub is basically a multiport repeater. A hub connects multiple wires coming from different branches, for example, the connector in a star topology that connects different stations. Hubs cannot filter data, so data packets are sent to all connected devices. In other words, a collision domain of all hosts connected through a hub remains one. Also, they do not have intelligence to find out the best path for data packets, which leads to inefficiencies and wastage.

Bridge

A bridge operates at the data link layer. A bridge is a repeater, with add on functionality of filtering content by reading the MAC addresses of source and destination. It is also used for interconnecting two LANs working on the same protocol. It has a single input and single output port, thus making it a two-port device.

Gateway

A gateway, as the name suggests, is a passage to connect two networks together that may work upon different networking models. They basically works as the messenger agents that take data from one system, interpret it, and transfer it to another system. Gateways are also called protocol converters and can operate at any network layer. Gateways are generally more complex than a switch or router.

Switch

A switch is a multi-port bridge with a buffer and a design that can boost its efficiency (large number of ports imply less traffic) and performance. A switch is a data link layer device. A switch can perform error checking before forwarding data that makes it very efficient as it does not forward packets that have errors and forward good packets selectively to correct port only. In other words, a switch divides collision domain of hosts, but the broadcast domain remains same.

Routers

A router is a device like a switch that routes data packets based on their IP addresses. A router is mainly a network layer device. Routers normally connect LANs and WANs together and have a dynamically updating routing table based on which they make decisions on routing the data packets. Routers divide broadcast domains of hosts connected through it.

Modem

A modem stands for **mo**dulator **dem**odulator. That means it modulates and demodulates the signal between the digital data of a computer and the analog signal of a telephone line. It converts the computer-generated digital signals of a computer into analog signals to enable their traveling via phone lines. It can be used as a dial-up for a LAN or to connect to an ISP. It can be both external, as in the device that connects to the USB or the serial port of a computer, or proprietary devices for handheld gadgets and other devices, as well as internal; in the form of add-in expansion cards for computers and PC cards for laptops.

Network host

A network host refers to any computer (or server) that is interlinked with another computer(s) or network devices through an Internet connection. Each host has its unique IP address, formed by the computer's local number and the particular number of the network it belongs to. The network host is responsible for storing data that will be transmitted to other computable devices, usually users' computers, called remote terminals.

Network protocol

The rules and conventions for communication between network devices are defined as a network protocol. It includes the characteristics of a network, such as access method, allowed physical topologies, types of cabling, and speed of data transfer.

Several types of computer network protocols have been developed for specific purposes and environments. Some major network protocols are described, including TCP, IP, POP, SMTP, HTTP, FTP, SSH, PPP, WAP, and VoIP.

Transmission control protocol

The **transmission control protocol** (**TCP**) is a communication protocol that computers use to communicate over a network. It divides a message into a stream of packets that are sent and then reassembled at the destination.

Internet protocol

The **Internet protocol** (**IP**) is an addressing protocol. It is always used together with TCP. The IP addresses the packet, routes them through different nodes and networks until they reach their final destination. TCP/IP is perhaps the most used standard protocol for connecting computer networks.

Internet protocol address

An Internet protocol (IP) address is the unique numerical address of a device in a computer network that uses the IP for communication. An IP address consists of four numbers; each can contain one to three digits. These numbers are separated with a single dot (.). These four numbers can range from 0 to 255. Some types of IP address are described next.

Public IP address

A public IP address is used for identification of a home network to the outside world. It is unique throughout the entire network. It is used on the Internet or other WAN. It is an IP address that your home or business router receives from your ISP. Public IP addresses are required for any publicly accessible network hardware, such as for your home router, as well as for the servers that host websites. It is sometimes called an Internet IP address.

Finding your public IP address

Go to Google and search for *ip*; it will show your public IP address:

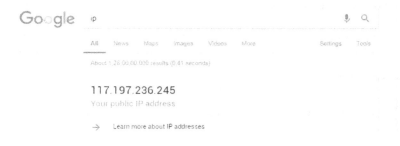

NOTE Websites for finding a public IP address are:

- *www.whatsmyip.org*
- *www.whatismyipaddress.com*
- *www.ipchicken.com*

Private IP address

A private IP address is used for identification of a network device inside the home network. Two or more separate networks can have same private IP addresses assigned to different computers. It is used on a LAN for computers not directly connected to the Internet. It is an IP address that is reserved for internal use behind a router or other **network address translation** (**NAT**) device, apart from the public. It is also known as a *local IP address*.

Finding your private IP address

For Windows OS users:

To open Command Prompt: Press the Windows key + *R*, then type *cmd* and click on OK:

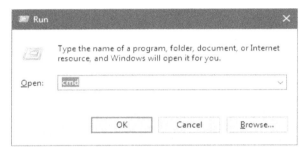

In the Command Prompt window, type *ipconfig* and press *Enter*:

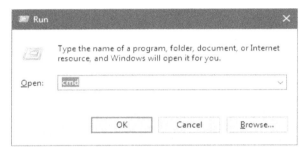

The IPv4 address shows the private IP address, like the preceding screenshot.

 To find a private IP address:

Linux users can launch the Terminal window and enter the command *hostname -I, ifconfig,* or *ip addr show.*

Mac OS users can use the command *ifconfig.*

Dynamic IP address

A dynamic IP address is an IP address that is automatically assigned to each connection of a network by a **Dynamic Host Configuration Protocol (DHCP)** server. It's called dynamic because it 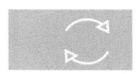 constantly changes. It is good for residential users and small business owners. The public IP address that gets assigned to the router of most home and business users by their ISPs is a dynamic IP address. The upload and download speed of a dynamic IP address is slower than the static IP address.

Static IP address

A static IP address is an IP address that was manually configured for a device. It's called static because it doesn't change. Routers, phones, tablets, desktops, laptops, and any  other device that can use an IP address can be configured to have a static IP address. It is widely used by web servers, e-mail servers, and other Internet servers. Also, it is used for **voice over IP (VOIP), VPN,** playing online games, or game hosting. The upload and download speed of a static IP address is faster than a dynamic IP address.

 Both private and public IP addresses are either dynamic or static, which means that, respectively, they either change or they don't.

The **Post Office Protocol (POP)** is used to receive incoming e-mails.

The **Simple Mail Transport Protocol (SMTP)** is used for sending and distributing outgoing e-mails.

Hypertext Transfer Protocol

The **Hypertext Transfer Protocol (HTTP)** is used to transfer a hypertext between two or more computers. Generally, it is used by a web server to allow web pages to be shown in a web browser. Hypertext is the text that is coded using the language called HTML. HTTP is based on the client/server principles, for example, https://www.google.co.in.

Hypertext Markup Language (HTML) is a standardized system for tagging text files to achieve font, color, graphic, and hyperlink effects on World Wide Web pages. It defines the structure and layout of a web document by using a variety of tags and attributes.

Hyper Text Transfer Protocol Secure (HTTPS) is the secure version of HTTP, the protocol over which data is sent between your browser and the website that you are connected to.

File Transfer Protocol

The **File Transfer Protocol (FTP)** allows users to transfer files from one computer to another computer. Files that can be transferred may include program files, text files, and multimedia files, etc. This method of file transfer is faster than that using HTTP. With a free FTP client software (such as FileZilla, Cyberduck or Transmit) uploading/downloading a file is really easy through the Internet.

SSH protocol

The SSH protocol is a method for secure remote login from one computer to another. It is also known as *Secure Shell*. It provides several alternative options for strong authentication, and it protects the communications security and integrity with strong encryption. It is a secure alternative to the non-protected login protocols (such as Telnet). It is also used for interactive and automated file transfers.

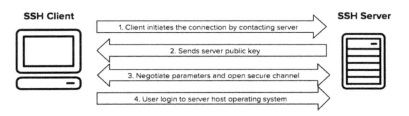

Point-to-point Protocol

The Point-to-point Protocol (PPP) provides a standard way to transport multiprotocol data over point-to-point links. It has three main components: a way to encapsulate multiprotocol datagrams; a Link Control Protocol to establish, configure, and test the data link connection; and a group of network control protocols that establish and configure different types of network layer protocols.

Wireless Application Protocol

The Wireless Application Protocol (WAP) is a communications protocol that is used for wireless data access through most mobile wireless networks.

VoIP

VoIP is the transmission of voice over IP networks. It is also referred to as IP telephony, Internet telephony, and Internet calling.

NOTE

A *Telnet* program runs on your computer and connects your PC to a server on the network. This enables you to control the server and communicate with other servers on the network. To start a Telnet session, you must log in to a server by entering a valid username and password. It is a common way to remotely control web servers.

Usenet is a collection of user-submitted notes or messages on various subjects that are posted to servers on a worldwide network. Each subject collection of posted notes is known as a newsgroup. The Network News Transfer Protocol (NNTP) is the predominant protocol used by computer clients and servers for managing the notes posted on Usenet newsgroups.

Gopher is a sort of rules used to search, retrieve, and display documents from remote sites. It is possible to initiate online connections with other systems through Gopher. It also operates on client/server principle.

Network port

A network port allows software applications to share hardware resources without interfering with each other. Port numbers are used to determine what protocol incoming traffic should be directed to. Each port number identifies a distinct service. The network ports are numbered from 0 to 65535. Port use is regulated by the Internet Corporation for Assigned Names and Numbers (ICANN).

Name of the service or protocol	Port number
File Transfer Protocol (FTP)	20, 21
Secure Shell (SSH)	22
Telnet	23
Simple Mail Transfer Protocol (SMTP)	25
Domain Name Server (DNS)	53
Dynamic Host Configuration Protocol (DHCP)	67, 68
Hypertext Transfer Protocol (HTTP)	80
Post Office Protocol (POP)	110
Network Time Protocol (NTP)	123
Internet Message Access Protocol (IMAP4)	143
Simple Network Management Protocol (SNMP)	161, 162
Lightweight Directory Access Protocol	389
HTTP with Secure Sockets Layer (SSL)	443

Network packet

A network packet is a basic unit of communication over a digital network. It is also called a datagram, a segment, a block, a cell or a frame or an IP packet, depending on the protocol used for the transmission of data. The IP requires a packet to have three basic elements: source, destination, and data. Packets are transmitted over packet switched networks, which are networks in which each message (i.e., data that is transmitted), such as an e-mail, web page, or program download, is cut up into a set small segments prior to transmission.

Each packet consists of three main parts: a header, a payload, and a footer.

A *header* consists of instructions regarding its packet data.

A *payload* is the actual data (i.e., part of the message) that the packet is delivering to the destination. It is also called as body or data area.

A *footer* contains several bits that tell the receiving device that it has reached the end of the packet. It is also called as a *trailer*. It may also include some type of error checking.

Ping

Ping is a network utility used to send a test packet, or echo packet, to a machine to find out whether the machine is reachable and how long the packet takes to reach the machine. Example of the *ping* command executed in the Command Prompt is shown as follows:

To open the Command Prompt, press the Windows key + *R*, then type *cmd* and click on OK.

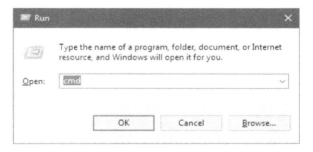

In the Command Prompt window, type *ping www.google.com* (any web address) and press *Enter*.

```
Select C:\Windows\system32\cmd.exe                      —    □    ×
Microsoft Windows [Version 10.0.14393]
(c) 2016 Microsoft Corporation. All rights reserved.

C:\Users\SRB>ping www.google.com

Pinging www.google.com [216.58.197.68] with 32 bytes of data:
Reply from 216.58.197.68: bytes=32 time=33ms TTL=56
Reply from 216.58.197.68: bytes=32 time=34ms TTL=56
Reply from 216.58.197.68: bytes=32 time=36ms TTL=56
Reply from 216.58.197.68: bytes=32 time=35ms TTL=56

Ping statistics for 216.58.197.68:
    Packets: Sent = 4, Received = 4, Lost = 0 (0% loss),
Approximate round trip times in milli-seconds:
    Minimum = 33ms, Maximum = 36ms, Average = 34ms

C:\Users\SRB>
```

The preceding screenshot shows you that a 32-byte echo packet was sent to the destination and returned. The TTL (time to live) item shows how many intermediary steps, or hops, the packet should take to the destination before giving up.

Tracert command not only tells you whether the packet got to its destination and how long it took, but also tells you all the intermediate hops it took to get there. You can use the *tracert* command in Command Prompt. Open the Command Prompt, type *tracert www.google.com* and press *Enter*.

Netstat is another network utility command shows you what connections your computer currently has. It is an abbreviation for *network status*. You can use it in the Command Prompt.

MAC address

A **MAC (Media Access Control)** address is a globally unique identifier assigned to network devices, and therefore, it is often referred to as hardware or physical address. The purpose of MAC addresses is to provide a unique hardware address or physical address for every node on a LAN or other network. A node is a point at which a computer or other device (e.g., a printer or router) is connected to the network. A MAC address is 48 bits in length.

How to find your MAC address

To open the Command Prompt: press the Windows key + *R*, then type *cmd* and click on OK.

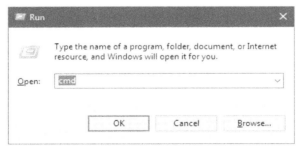

In the Command Prompt window, type *ipconfig/all* and press *Enter*.

```
Select C:\Windows\system32\cmd.exe                                      —    □    ×
Microsoft Windows [Version 10.0.14393]
(c) 2016 Microsoft Corporation. All rights reserved.

C:\Users\SRB>ipconfig/all

Windows IP Configuration

   Host Name . . . . . . . . . . . . : DESKTOP-CRMK5VG
   Primary Dns Suffix  . . . . . . . :
   Node Type . . . . . . . . . . . . : Hybrid
   IP Routing Enabled. . . . . . . . : No
   WINS Proxy Enabled. . . . . . . . : No

Ethernet adapter Ethernet:

   Connection-specific DNS Suffix  . :
   Description . . . . . . . . . . . : Intel(R) Ethernet Connection (2) I219-V
   Physical Address. . . . . . . . . : 40-8D-5C-B9-90-6C
   DHCP Enabled. . . . . . . . . . . : No
   Autoconfiguration Enabled . . . . : Yes
   Link-local IPv6 Address . . . . . : fe80::48c:c62a:9498:21af%12(Preferred)
   IPv4 Address. . . . . . . . . . . : 192.168.1.100(Preferred)
   Subnet Mask . . . . . . . . . . . : 255.255.255.0
   Default Gateway . . . . . . . . . : fe80::1e5f:2bff:fe3f:32b8%12
                                       192.168.1.1
   DHCPv6 IAID . . . . . . . . . . . : 37784924
   DHCPv6 Client DUID. . . . . . . . : 00-01-00-01-20-39-88-C0-40-8D-5C-B9-90-6C
   DNS Servers . . . . . . . . . . . : 8.8.8.8
                                       8.8.4.4
```

You can see your MAC address in the Physical Address field, as seen in the preceding screenshot.

Domain Name System

A **Domain Name System (DNS)** is used to translate hostname or Internet domain into IP addresses and vice versa.

When you visit *www.google.com* in a browser, your computer uses DNS to retrieve the website's IP address of *213.58.203.132*. Without DNS, you would only be able to visit our website (or any website) by visiting its IP address directly, such as *http://216.58.203.132*.

Finding the IP address of a domain name

For Windows OS users:
To open the Command Prompt, press the Windows key + *R*, then type *cmd* and click on **OK**:

In the Command Prompt window, type *nslookup* and press *Enter*.

Type the website or domain (e.g., www.google.com) name and press Enter:

```
Select C:\Windows\system32\cmd.exe - nslookup                    —   □   ×
Microsoft Windows [Version 10.0.14393]
(c) 2016 Microsoft Corporation. All rights reserved.

C:\Users\SRB>nslookup
Default Server:  google-public-dns-a.google.com
Address:  8.8.8.8

> www.google.com
Server:  google-public-dns-a.google.com
Address:  8.8.8.8

Non-authoritative answer:
Name:    www.google.com
Addresses:  2404:6800:4009:802::2004
            216.58.203.132

>
```

The IP address of that website shows in the **Addresses** field, as shown in the preceding screenshot.

Firewall

A firewall is a piece of hardware or software that prevents malware and malicious attacks from entering a computer or a network of computers through the Internet. Simply, the firewall monitors all this information traffic to allow "good data" in, but block "bad data" from entering your computer.

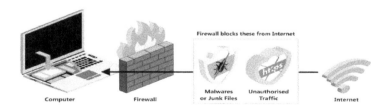

The three firewall scanning methods are packet filtering, proxy service, and stateful inspection.

Packet filtering blocks the incoming packet of information (small chunk of data) if it is flagged by the pre-determined security filters.

Proxy service operates at the application layer of the firewall, where both ends of a connection are forced to conduct the session through the proxy.

Stateful inspection doesn't rely on the memory-intensive examination of all information packets. The firewall compares information being transferred to the copy relevant to that transfer held in the database; if the comparison yields a positive match, the information is allowed through, otherwise it is denied.

Proxy server

A proxy server is an intermediary server between a client and the real server, which is used to filter or cache requests made by the client. It intercepts all requests to the real server to see whether it can fulfill the requests itself. If not, it forwards the request to the real server.

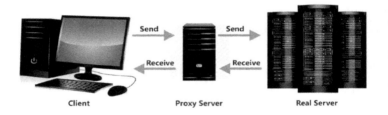

There are many different types of proxy servers. Some common types of proxy servers are as follows:

Anonymous proxy servers are used to conceal your information. When you go to request something from the web page, the web page gets the IP address of the proxy server that you're using instead of your own. The server cannot access your IP address, and the communication between you and the proxy server is encrypted.

Transparent proxy servers are used to forward your request to the resource that you want without concealing any of your information.

Reverse proxy servers are used to pass requests from the Internet, through a firewall to isolated, private networks. It prevents Internet clients from having direct, unmonitored access to sensitive data residing on content servers on an isolated network, or intranet. It benefits the web server rather than its clients.

CHAPTER 4

Hacking Skills and Tools

Hacking skills

Hacking is among the most skilled information technology disciplines; it requires a wide knowledge of digital networking, programming, virtualization, security concepts, web applications, and so on. A hacker should also know how to operate Linux (Kali Linux) and other operating systems.

Programming language

It is a vocabulary and set of grammatical rules for instructing a computer or computing device to perform specific tasks. Examples of programming language include BASIC, C, C++, COBOL, Java, FORTRAN, Ada, Pascal, PHP, and so on

Generally, programming languages are divided into two categories according to their interpretation, low-level language and high-level language.

Low-level language

A low-level language is designed to operate and handle the entire hardware and instructions set architecture of a computer directly. It considered to be closer to computers. The prime function is to operate, manage, and manipulate the computing hardware and components.

There are two types of low-level languages: machine language (machine code) and assembly language

Machine language (machine code)

Machine language was the first type of programming language to be developed. It is basically the only language that a computer can understand. It is represented inside the computer by a string of binary digits (bits) 0 and 1. Here, 0 stands for the absence of an electric pulse and 1 for the presence of an electric pulse.

Assembly language

Assembly language was developed to overcome some of the many inconveniences of machine language. In this language, operation codes and operands are given in the form of alphanumeric symbols instead of 0s and 1s. These alphanumeric symbols can have maximum up to five-letter combination, for example, ADD for addition, SUB for subtraction, START, LABEL. Because of this feature, it is also known as a "symbolic programming language."

High-level language (HLL)

A high-level language is any programming language that enables the development of a program in a much more user-friendly programming context and is generally independent of the computer's hardware architecture. It has a higher level of abstraction from the computer and focuses more on the programming logic, rather than the underlying hardware components, such as memory addressing and register utilization.

Language translator

A language translator translates instructions that are written in the source code to object code, that is, from high-level language or assembly language into machine language. It is also called a language processor.

Depending on the programming languages, the language translator is divided into three types: *compiler*, *interpreter*, and *assembler*.

Assembler

An assembler translates assembly language program (source codes) into a machine language program (object codes). The original assembly language program codes are called source codes, and after translation, the final machine language program codes are called object codes. It is the translator program for a low-level programming language.

Compiler

A compiler translates a high-level language program into a machine language program. While translating, it checks the syntax (grammar of the source code) and translates it into the object code in a single attempt. If any error is found, the compiler produces syntax errors and causes of the errors. The source code file must be syntax error-free for complete compilation process. Examples of compliers are C, C++, Visual Basic, Java, and so on

Interpreter

An interpreter translates a high-level language program into a machine language program, one instruction at a time. Unlike the compiler, it translates and executes one statement at a time before moving to another. If any error is encountered, the translation is halted and an error message is displayed. Examples of interpreters are Python, BASIC, Ruby, and so on

 Debugging is the process of finding and fixing bugs (errors) within the program that prevent correct operation of computer software or a system.

Programming language for hackers

Programming language	Description	Use in hacking purpose
HTML	Writing web pages	It helps understanding web actions, response, and logic. Writing and interpreting HTML makes it easy for you to identify and exploit weaknesses in the code.
JavaScript	Client-side scripting language	JavaScript code is executed on the client browser. It can be used to read saved cookies and perform cross-site scripting and so on.
PHP	Server-side scripting language	It is used to process HTML forms and performs other custom tasks. It is also used for modification settings on a web server and makes the server vulnerable to attacks.
SQL	Database scripting	It is used basically for SQL injection, to bypass web application login algorithms that are weak, delete data from the database, and so on

Python Ruby Bash Perl	High-level programming languages	These programming languages are used for developing automation tools and scripts.
C and C++		C is used in system programming, and C ++ is used in system object programming. Both are used for writing exploits and shell codes.
Java C Sharp Visual Basic VBScript		Java is used in Internet-oriented programming, C Sharp is used as common language infrastructure, and Visual Basic and VBScript (only in Microsoft Windows OS) are used in component object model (COM) programming.

Hacking tools

Hacking tools are a pre-programmed tool/software to assist with hacking, or a piece of software that can be used for hacking purposes.

Commonly used hacking tools

Hacking tool	Description
Kali Linux	It is a security-focused operating system packed with distribution and interface tools. You can run off a CD or USB drive, anywhere. With its security toolkit, you can crack Wi-Fi passwords, create fake networks, and test other vulnerabilities.
Metasploit	It is used for pentesting or hacking a framework. It is essentially a computer security project (framework) that provides the user with vital information regarding known security vulnerabilities and helps to formulate penetration testing and **Intrusion Detection Systems (IDS)** testing plans, strategies, and methodologies for exploitation.

Wireshark	It is a web vulnerability scanner. It essentially captures data packets in a network in real time and then displays the data in a human-readable format.
Burp Suite	It is used to map out and list the different parameters and pages of a website by examining the cookies and initiating connections with applications residing in the website. It is basically a web application vulnerability scanner.
Nessus	It is a vulnerability scanner. It can scan multiple types of vulnerabilities that include remote access flaw detection, misconfiguration alert, denial-of-services against TCP/IP stack, preparation of **Payment Card Industry Data Security Standard (PCI DSS)** audits, malware detection, sensitive data searches, and so on
Netsparker	It is a web application scanner that finds flaws such as SQL injection and local file induction, suggesting remedial actions in a read-only and safe way.
Angry IP Scanner	It is used to scan IP addresses and ports to look for doorways into a user's system. It is an open source and cross-platform software and one of the most efficient hacking tools present in the market.
NetStumbler	It is a Windows tool to find open wireless access points. It is used for wardriving, verifying network configurations, finding locations with a poor network, detecting unauthorized access points, and more.
Aircrack	It cracks vulnerable wireless connections. It is powered by WEP WPA and WPA2 encryption keys.
Nmap	Network mapper is used to scan ports and map networks. It uses raw IP packets in creative ways to determine what hosts are available on the network, what services (application name and version) those hosts are providing information about, what operating systems (fingerprinting) and what type and version of packet filters/ firewalls are being used by the target.

SQLmap	It is an open source penetration testing tool that automates the process of detecting and exploiting SQL injection flaws and taking over of database servers. It can perform six SQL injection techniques: Boolean-based blind, time-based blind, error-based, UNION, query-based, stacked queries, and out-of-band. It has full support for MySQL, Oracle, PostgreSQL, Microsoft SQL Server, Microsoft Access, IBM DB2, SQLite, Firebird, Sybase, SAP MaxDB, HSQLDB, and Informix database management systems.
Cain and Abel	It is a password recovery and hacking tool primarily used for Microsoft Windows OS. It helps with password recovery by cracking encrypted passwords using a few brute force methods such as the dictionary method. It can also record VoIP conversations and recover wireless network keys.
John the Ripper	It is a password cracking tool that uses dictionary attacks. It can also be used to perform a variety of alterations to dictionary attacks.
Medusa	It is an online brute-force, speedy, parallel password cracking hacking tool.
PuTTY	It is an open-source terminal emulator, serial console, and network file transfer application.

These common hacking tools are used by both cyber criminals and ethical hackers to infiltrate or to protect a system, respectively. The use of the aforementioned hacking tools and many more tools are described in the upcoming chapters.

CHAPTER 5

Virtualization and Kali Linux

Virtualization

Virtualization refers to running multiple operating systems on a computer system simultaneously. Desktop users are to be able to run applications meant for different operating systems without having to switch computers or reboot into a different system. Administrators of servers are able to run different operating systems, but perhaps, more essentially, it offers a way to segment a large system into many smaller parts, allowing the server to be used more efficiently by a number of different users or applications with different needs.

The technology behind virtualization is known as a virtual machine monitor (VMM) or virtual manager, which separates compute environments from the actual physical infrastructure. Virtualization can be categorized into different layers: desktop, server, file, storage, and network.

Virtual machine

A virtual machine (VM) is a tightly isolated software container with an operating system and application inside. It is also known as a virtual computer system. Each self-contained VM is completely independent. Putting multiple VMs on a single computer enables several operating systems and applications to run on just one physical server, or "host".

 Some major virtualization software are *VMware Workstation, VirtualBox*, etc.

Installation of VMware Workstation

1. Download the latest VMware Workstation from *www.vmware.com*:

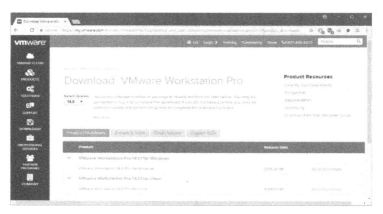

2. After downloading it, open (double-click) the VMware Workstation Pro launcher.

3. Click on Next and accept the terms in the License Agreement by checking the empty box:

4. Click on Next of all the setup wizard, and when you ready to install, click on **Install**:

5. After the installation is complete, click on **Finish**. An icon shows on the desktop as **VMware Workstation Pro** like the following screenshot:

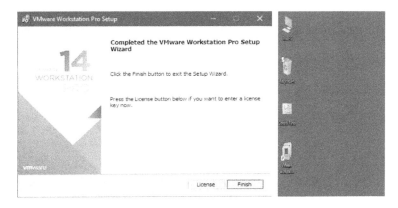

VMware Workstation Window

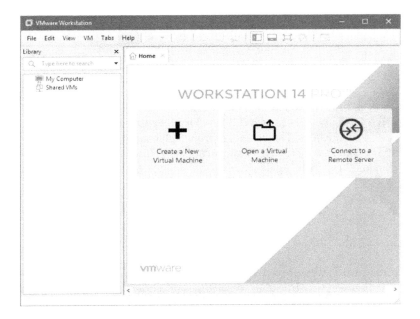

What is Linux?

It is a free and open source software operating system, based on UNIX that was created in 1991 by *Linus Torvalds*. It is used for computers, servers, mainframes, mobile devices, and embedded devices. *Tux* the penguin is the mascot of Linux.

> **NOTE** UNIX is a family of multitasking, multiuser computer operating systems that develop from the original *AT&T Unix*, development starting in the *1970s* at the *Bell Labs* research center by *Ken Thompson*, *Dennis Ritchie*, and others.

Linux distributions

A distribution of Linux includes the kernel, system utilities, programs, and tools for downloading, installing and uninstalling OS updates.

> **NOTE** A *kernel* is the central OS component and the bridge between a software application and its data.

Linux is distributed worldwide under a General Public License GNU. GNU stands for GNUs not Unix, which makes the term a recursive acronym (an acronym in which one of the letters stands for the acronym itself). There are many Linux distributions or "distros" around the world.

> **NOTE** Linux distributions may be *ready-to-use* or *source code* that you must compile locally during initial installation.

Community-developed distributions include *Debian, Slackware* and *Gentoo*. Commercial distributions include *Fedora* by Red Hat, *openSUSE* from SUSE, and *Ubuntu* from Canonical.

BOSS (Bharat Operating System Solutions) *Linux* is a free/open source GNU/Linux distribution developed by the Center for Development of Advanced Computing (C-DAC), Chennai.

Live Linux distributions (live CD/USB)

Linux distribution can be booted from removable storage media such as optical discs or USB flash drives, instead of being installed on and booted from a hard disk drive. It acts like a *live Linux distribution.*

Some primary live Linux distributions are Knoppix, Puppy Linux, Devil-Linux, and SliTaz GNU/Linux. Other live Linux distributions have a conventional form, which is a network-based or removable-media image intended to be used only for installation; such distributions include SUSE, Ubuntu, Linux Mint, MEPIS, and Fedora.

Linux architecture

Linux architecture consist four layers, such as hardware, kernel, shell, and utilities.

Hardware consists of all peripheral devices such as RAM, HDD, CPU, etc.

Kernel is the core component of the operating system, interacts directly with hardware.

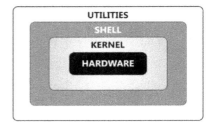

Shell is the interface to kernel, hiding complexity of kernel's functions from users. It takes commands from the user and executes kernel's functions.

Utilities provide the user most of the functionalities of an operating systems.

Linux directory structure

Linux directory structure can be described in root file system or root (/) directory.

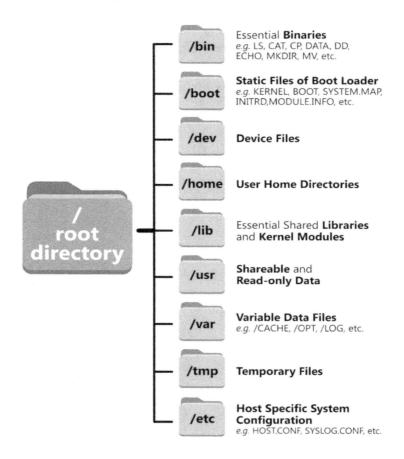

/bin	Essential **Binaries** *e.g.* LS, CAT, CP, DATA, DD, ECHO, MKDIR, MV, etc.
/boot	**Static Files of Boot Loader** *e.g.* KERNEL, BOOT, SYSTEM.MAP, INITRD,MODULE.INFO, etc.
/dev	**Device Files**
/home	**User Home Directories**
/lib	Essential Shared **Libraries** and **Kernel Modules**
/usr	**Shareable** and **Read-only Data**
/var	**Variable Data Files** *e.g.* /CACHE, /OPT, /LOG, etc.
/tmp	**Temporary Files**
/etc	**Host Specific System Configuration** *e.g.* HOST.CONF, SYSLOG.CONF, etc.

/ root directory

Basic file management

A file is used to store data, and it is simply described by a sequence of bytes. A directory (or folder) is a collection of files and other directories. Directories are organized in a hierarchy, with the root directory at the top. The root directory is referred to as / (absolute) symbol. A user can refer to files in directories and sub-directories by separating their names with /, for example, /*home/srb/books*.

File extension: A file extension indicates the type of the file. A filename always has an extension, beginning with a dot. Linux operating system ignores the file extensions. Only a few specific programs use extensions to identify the type of a file. Some file extensions are listed in the following table:

File extension	Refers to
.bin	Binary file to be executed
.deb	A Debian package file
.dsc	A Debian source information file
.iso	An image (copy) of a CD-ROM or DVD
.txt	A plain ASCII text file
.gif	Graphics interchange format image
.jpg	Joint Photographic Experts Group image
.gz	Compressed file
.tar	Unix *tape archive* file
.tgz	Compressed archive file

Kali Linux

Kali Linux is a Debian-derived Linux distribution, especially used by ethical hackers for digital forensics and penetration testing. It is developed by Offensive Security Limited. It contains a set of tools divided by the categories. You can download Kali Linux, watch video tutorials, join the forum, and many more from *www.kali.org* (the official website).

 NOTE *BackTrack* is the old version of Kali Linux distribution.

Installing Kali Linux using VMware Workstation

Nowadays, most of the users preferred to install Kali Linux (as a secondary operating system) in a Windows OS (like Windows 10,

8.1, or 7 as primary operating system) environment. So, you can learn how to install a Kali Linux in a Windows 10 by using VMware Workstation.

Follow the steps:

1. Before installation, first you have to download Kali Linux from the website *www.kali.org/downloads*:

2. Choose your OS and download it from the aforementioned website. In this installation, we use Kali Linux 64-bit VMware VM, which you can download from *https://www.offensive-security.com/kali-linux-vmware-virtualbox-image-download/*:

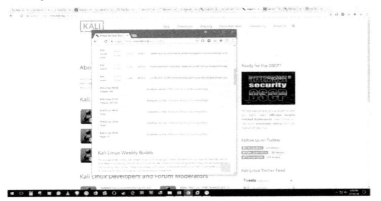

3. Download **Kali Linux 64 bit VM** using Torrent.

4. After finishing the download, open the downloaded folder that contains **Kali Linux 64 bit VM**, as shown in the following screenshot:

5. Now, open the application file (Open Virtualization Format Distribution Package) by double-clicking:

6. Click on **Import** to install Kali Linux through VMware Workstation.

7. After installation is completed, **Kali Linux** opens in a new tab of VMware Workstation, just like the following screenshot:

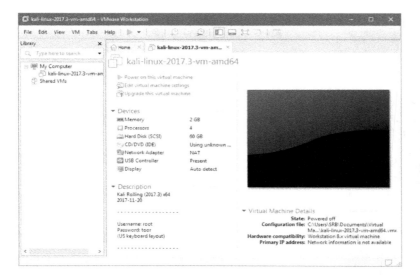

Using Kali Linux for the first time

Turn on

1. Open VMware Workstation and click on kali-linux (following is the screenshot of my computer). It will open in a new tab as follows:

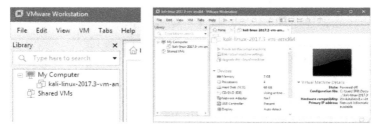

2. Click on **Power on this virtual machine** to turn on Kali Linux.

3. After booting up (or turning on), you can enter *root* as the username and click on **Next**. After that, enter *toor* as the

password and click on **Sign In**. Because, the default username and password are *root* and *toor,* respectively:

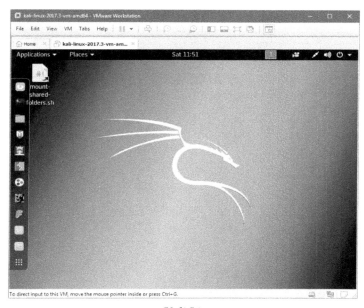

Kali Linux

Turn Off and Restart

Simply, click on the turn off button ⏻ (on the upper-right side of Kali Linux window) to open the turn off menu and again click on turn off button ⏻ (on bottom-right corner of turn off menu). Then, click on **Power Off** for turn off or click on Restart to **restart** Kali Linux:

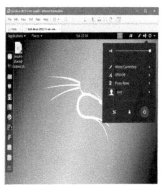
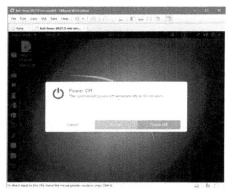

Kali Linux tools

There are so many pre-installed hacking tools and applications in Kali Linux. These tools are characterized by their uses.

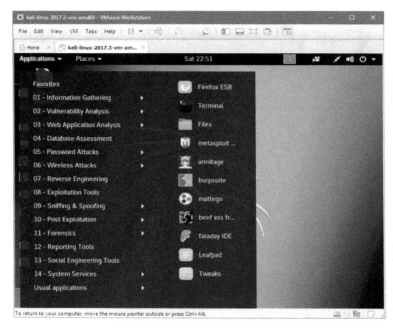

As you can see from the preceding screenshot, the applications or tools are characterized by information gathering, vulnerability analysis, web application analysis, database assessment, password attacks, wireless attacks, reverse engineering, exploitation tools, sniffing and spoofing, post-exploitation, forensics, reporting tools, social engineering tools, system services, and usual applications.

The major hacking applications and tools of Kali Linux are briefly described in separate chapters in this book.

Kali Linux console Terminal

There are two different way to manage files in Linux, such as Terminal (**command-line interface – CLI**) and File manager (**graphical user interface – GUI**). Most Linux users consider the Linux console Terminal to be faster and more efficient than the GUI mode.

A Terminal is a text input/output environment. A Linux console Terminal is one of the system consoles provided in the Linux kernel. It acts as the medium for input and output operations for a Linux system. It is similar to command line in Microsoft Windows, but it differs in that it can perform any operation on the system.

Major functions of Linux console Terminal are as follows:

- Extensive system monitoring.
- Extensive, system-wide configuration and administration.
- File and folder administration.
- Ability to access, transfer, and share data between machines.

Lunching the Terminal

To open the Terminal on desktop: Simply open the **Terminal** by using the Terminal button from the sidebar and a blank Terminal window shows:

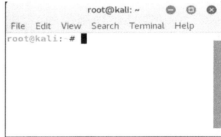

To open the Terminal on a desired location: Go to the location where you want to open the Terminal and right-click in the blank space, then click on **Open in Terminal**:

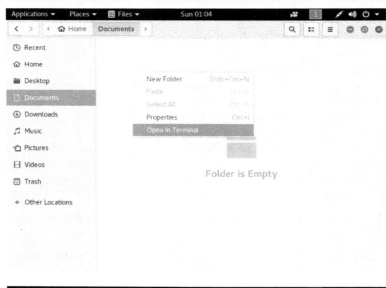

Parts of the Terminal window

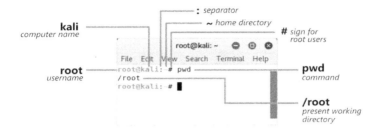

Keyboard shortcuts for Linux Terminal

Shortcut	Action
Ctrl + Shift + C	Copy
Ctrl + Shift + V	Paste
Ctrl + Shift + N	New window
Ctrl + Shift + W	Close window
F11	View Terminal full screen
Shift + PgUp	Scroll up
Shift + PgDn	Scroll down
Shift + Home	Scroll to the beginning
Shift + End	Scroll to the end
Ctrl + Shift + T	New tab
Ctrl + Shift + Q	Close tab
Ctrl + PgUp	Next tab
Ctrl + PgDn	Previous tab
Alt + n	Where n is a number in the range of 1 to 9, go to tab n

Working with some common commands

Present working directory (pwd)

The currently browsing directory is referred to as the present working directory. When you boot up your PC, you log on to the home directory. To determine the directory you are presently working on, use the command *pwd*:

```
root@kali: ~
File  Edit  View  Search  Terminal  Help
root@kali:~# pwd
/root
root@kali:~#
```

The preceding screenshot shows that /**root** is the directory we are currently working on.

Changing directories (cd)

To change your current directory, you can use the *cd* command, for example, *cd /tem*.

Refer the following example. In the following screenshot, we moved from directory */tmp* to */bin* to */usr* and then back to */tmp*:

```
root@kali: /tmp
File  Edit  View  Search  Terminal  Help
root@kali:~/Documents# cd /tmp
root@kali:/tmp# cd /bin
root@kali:/bin# cd /usr
root@kali:/usr# cd /tmp
root@kali:/tmp#
```

Navigating to the home directory (cd ~)

To navigate to the home directory, you can use the *cd* or *cd ~* command. In the following screenshot, we navigate to home directory from the /Desktop directory:

Do not forget to put a space between *cd* and ~; Otherwise, you will get an error.

Navigating to the root directory (cd /)

To navigate to the root directory, you can use the *cd /* command. In the following screenshot, we navigate to the root directory from the /**Desktop** directory:

> **TiP**
>
> Do not forget to put a space between *cd* and /; Otherwise, you will get an error.

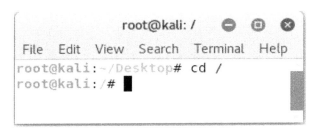

Listing files (ls)

To list a file in any directory, you can use the *ls* command. In the following screenshot, we can the list of files in the home directory:

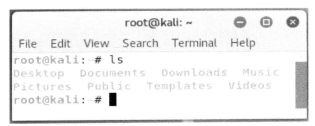

Command	Action
ls -R	Lists files in sub-directories as well
ls -a	Lists hidden files as well
ls -al	Lists files and directories with detailed information like permissions, size, owner, etc.

Shutting down (shutdown)

To shut down and restart, you can use the following commands:

Command	Action
shutdown	To shut down in next minute
shutdown -h now	To shut down now
shutdown -r now	To reboot or restart now
shutdown -h +5	To shut down the computer in 5 minutes time. *you can set the time limit as per your choice.*
shutdown -c	To cancel a shutdown

Kali Linux commands (working in the Terminal)

File/Directory basics

Command	Action
ls	List files
cp	Copy files
rename	Rename files
mv	Move or rename files or directories
mmv	Mass move and rename files
rm	Delete files
ln	Link files
cd	Change a directory
pwd	Print current directory name
mkdir	Create a directory (or folder)
rmdir	Delete a directory (or folder)

File viewing

Command	Action
cat	View files
less	Display output one screen at a time
head	Output the first part of files
tail	Output the last part of file
nl	Number lines and write files

File creation and editing

Command	Action
vi	Text editor
umask	Users file creation mask

File properties

Command	Action
stat	Display file or filesystem status
wc	Count bytes/words/lines
du	Measure disk usage
file	Identify file types
touch	Change file timestamps
chown	Change file owner
chgrp	Change file group
chmod	Change file protections or access permissions
lsattr	List advanced file attributes

File location

Command	Action
find	Search for files that meet desired criteria
locate	Find files
slocate	Locate files via index
which	Locate commands
whereis	Locate standard files

File text manipulation

Command	Action
grep	Search text for matching lines
cut	Divide a file into several parts or *extract columns*
paste	Merge lines of files or *append columns*
tr	Translate characters
sort	Sort lines
uniq	Locate identical lines
tee	Copy *stdin* to a file and to *stdout* simultaneously or *redirect output to multiple files*

File compression

Command	Action
gzip	Compress files (GNU Zip)
bzip2	Compress files (BZip2)

File comparison

Command	Action
diff	Display the differences between two files
diff3	Show differences among three files
comm	Compare two sorted files line-by-line
cmp	Compare files byte-by-byte

Disks and filesystems

Command	Action
df	Show free disk space
mount	Make a disk accessible
fsck	Check a disk for errors
sync	Flush disk caches

Processes

Command	Action
ps	List all processes or *process status*
clear	Clear the Terminal screen
uptime	View the system load
top	Monitor processes
free	Display free memory
kill	Terminate processes
nice	Set process priorities
renice	Change process priorities
shutdown	Shutdown or restart Linux

Scheduling jobs

Command	Action
sleep	Wait for some time
watch	Run programs at set intervals
crontab	Schedule a command to run at a later time

Hosts

Command	Action
uname	Print system information
hostname	Print the system's hostname
ifconfig	Set/display network information
ifdown	Stop a network interface
ifup	Start a network interface up
dig	Look up DNS
ping	Check whether host is reachable
traceroute	View network path to a host
who	Print all usernames currently logged in

Networking

Command	Action
ssh	Securely log into remote hosts
scp	Securely copy files between hosts
sftp	Securely copy files between hosts
ftp	Copy files between hosts
mozilla	Web browser
telnet	Used to communicate with another host using the telnet protocol
wget	Retrieve web pages or files via HTTP, HTTPS, or FTP
write	Send messages to a terminal or *to another user*

Other useful commands

Command	Action
tar	Read/write tape archives
rsync	Remote file copy (synchronize file trees)
strace	Trace system calls and signals
history	Shows all the commands that you have used in the past for the current terminal session
cat > filename	Creates a new file
cat filename	Displays the file content
cat file file2 > file3	Joins two files (file1, file2) and stores the output in a new file (file3)
apt-get	Command used to install and update packages
mail -s 'subject' -c 'cc-address' -b 'bcc-address' 'to-address'	Command to send an e-mail
mail -s "Subject" to-address < Filename	Command to send an e-mail with attachment

Connecting to a remote server

SSH (or Secure Shell) is used to log into a remote machine and execute commands and it supports tunneling, forwarding TCP ports. It can transfer files using the associated SSH file transfer

(SFTP) or secure copy (SCP) protocols. SSH uses the client-server model.

SSH on Linux

In Linux, SSH provides a text-based interface by spawning a remote shell. After connecting, all commands you type in your local Terminal are sent to the remote server and executed there.

To connect to a remote server and open a shell session there, you can use the *ssh* command in the Terminal of Linux. The simplest form assumes that your username on your local machine is the same as that on the remote server. If this is true, you can connect using:

```
ssh remote_host
```

If your username is different on the remoter server, you need to pass the remote user's name as follows:

```
ssh username@remote_host
```

If you are connecting to a new host for the first time, you will see a message that looks as follows:

```
The authenticity of host '111.111.11.111 (111.111.11.111)' can't be established.
ECDSA key fingerprint is fd:fd:d4:f9:77:fe:73:84:e1:55:00:ad:d6:6d:22:fe.
Are you sure you want to continue connecting (yes/no)? yes
```

Type *yes* to accept the authenticity of the remote host.

If you are using password authentication, you will be prompted for the password for the remote account here. If you are using SSH keys, you will be prompted for your private key's passphrase if one is set; otherwise, you will be logged in automatically.

To exit into your local session, simply type: *exit*

Running a single command on a remote server

To run a single command on a remote server instead of spawning a shell session, you can add the command after the connection information, as follows:

> ssh username@remote_host command_to_run

This command will connect to the remote host, authenticate with your credentials, and execute the command you specified. The connection will immediately close afterwards.

SSH on Windows

PuTTY is an SSH and telnet client, developed originally by Simon Tatham for the Windows platform. It supports several network protocols, including SCP, SSH, Telnet, rlogin, and raw socket connection. It can also connect to a serial port.

You can download PuTTY from *https://www.chiark.greenend. org.uk/~sgtatham/putty/latest.html.*

Running PuTTY and connecting to a server

If you selected to create a desktop icon during installation, you can start the software simply by double-clicking on the icon. Otherwise, open the software from the Windows Start menu:

When the software starts, a window titled PuTTY Configuration should open. This window has a configuration pane on the left, a Host Name (or IP address) field and other options in the middle, and a pane for saving session profiles in the lower-right area. For simple use, all you need to do is to enter the domain name or IP address of the host you want to connect to in the Host Name (or IP address) field and click on Open (or press *Enter*). It will establish the connection with the Linux machine and ask you to enter the username and password. After entering the username and password, you will be able to execute commands on the target machine.

CHAPTER 6

Social Engineering and Reverse Social Engineering

Social engineering

Social engineering is the art of manipulating people so that they give away confidential information, such as your passwords or bank information, or access your computer to secretly install malicious software. The objective of a social engineer is to trick someone into providing valuable information or access to that information. The major social engineering attacks are taken by the hackers who are able to blend in and act to be a part of the organization. This ability to blend in is commonly referred to as the *art of manipulation*.

Types of social engineering attacks

Social engineering can be classified into two types: *human-based* and *computer-based*

Human-based social engineering

Human-based social engineering refers to person-to-person interaction to retrieve the confidential information. It can include the following methods of attacks:

- **Impersonating an employee or a valid user:** The hacker pretends to be an employee or a valid user on the system to gain confidential information.

- **Posing as an important user:** The hacker pretends to be an executive or high-level manager who needs assistance to retrieve the computer system or files.

- **Using a third person:** The hacker pretends to have permission from an authorized source by using the third-person approach to use a system.

- **Calling technical support:** The hacker calls the helpdesk and technical support personnel for assistance and to gain some important information.

- **Shoulder surfing:** The hacker can gather confidential information such as system password by watching over a person's shoulder while they log in to the system.

- **Dumpster diving:** The hacker looks in the trash for information on pieces of paper or computer printouts, and they can often find passwords, filenames, or other pieces of confidential information.

- **Tailgating** or **piggybacking**: This is a physical security breach in which an unauthorized person (or hacker) follows an authorized person to enter a secured premise.

Computer-based social engineering

Computer-based social engineering refers to having computer software that attempts to retrieve the confidential information. It can include the following methods of attacks:

- **Phishing**: It involves sending an e-mail, usually posing as a bank, credit card company, or other financial organization. This type of e-mails often consists a link or an attachment that will redirect to install a malware. This method is meant to trick the recipient into sharing personal or financial information. By this method, the hacker is then able to capture this information and use it for financial gain or to perpetrate other attacks.

- **Pretexting:** It is performed by an individual by lying to other for gaining confidential data. It often involves a scam where the hacker pretends to need information in order to confirm the identity of the person he is talking to.

- **Online scams** (baiting): It is performed by scammers who may offer users free downloads of music and movie, if users surrender their login credentials to a certain site. Sometimes, the scammer uses fake websites that make free offers or other special deals that can bait a victim to enter a username and password, so that they can use their login credentials to gain information in the website form.

- **Scareware:** It is designed to trick a user into buying and downloading excessive and potentially dangerous software, such as a fake antivirus protection, antispyware software, a firewall application, or a registry cleaner. In reality, no problems were solved by these software (scareware), and it may actually contain real malware that will help the hacker to gaining the access to the system.

 NOTE *URL obfuscation* consists of hiding a fake URL in what appears to be a legitimate website address.

Reverse social engineering

In social engineering attacks, the attacker goes to the victim to obtain information. In reverse social engineering, however, the victim unwittingly goes to the attacker. A reverse social engineering attack is where an attacker makes himself a point of help to a victim. The victim will think of the attacker as a trustworthy person because he is offering help to solve the problem. For example, a hacker can impersonate a helpdesk employee or support assistant and get the user to give them information, such as a password.

The three parts of reverse social engineering attacks are *sabotage*, *advertising*, and *assisting*. The hacker *sabotages* a network, causing a problem arise. That hacker then *advertises* that he is the appropriate contact to fix the problem, and then, when he *assists* to fix the network problem, he requests certain bits of information from the employees and gets what he really came for.

Countermeasures of social engineering and reverse social engineering

- Secure your computing devices with a strong password.
- Use genuine antivirus or Internet security software.
- Do not open any e-mails from untrusted sources.
- Do not give offers from strangers the benefit of the doubt.

- Do not share your ID and password with anybody else in any case.
- Reject requests for help or offers of help.
- Delete any request for financial information or passwords.
- Set your spam filters to high (or maximum) in the e-mail setting.
- Read your company's privacy policy.

Social engineering toolkit (SET) - Kali Linux tools

Social engineering toolkit (**SET**) is an open source penetration testing framework designed for social engineering. SET has a number of custom attack vectors that allow you to make a believable attack in a fraction of time.

How to open a tool from SET

1. To open SET, go to **Applications** > **Social Engineering Tools** > Click on the **SET** icon, as shown in the following screenshot:

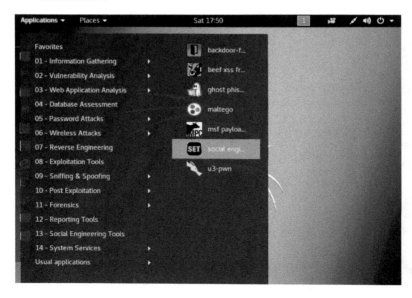

2. It will ask whether you agree with the terms of usage, as shown in the following screenshot. Type *y* to agree the terms and press *Enter* to open SET:

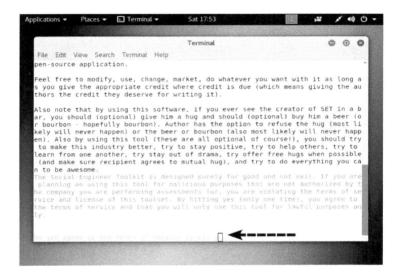

3. Type *1* and press *Enter* to open social engineering attacks tools, as shown in the following screenshot:

Now you can type the number (1 to 11) from the menu and press *Enter* to perform the specific social engineering attack as you want.

Mass mailer attack

A social engineer will attack a network by sending e-mails to mass number of e-mail addresses (individual e-mail addresses or company e-mail addresses) and see who will respond or run the malicious attachment you sent with it. The *Mass Mailer Attack* tool of Kali Linux allows you to send e-mails to multiple individual in a list.

Follow the steps:First, you have to create a list of e-mail IDs on Kali Linux such as the following screenshots.

1. To create a text file in Kali Linux, go to **Applications** > **Usual applications** > **Accessories** > **Text Editor**. A blank text file (named as **Untitled Document 1**) will open. In this text file, you have to enter some e-mail IDs and save it. In the following example, I save the text file on desktop and named as *email-list.txt*. So, here, the path to the file to import into SET is */root/Desktop/email-list.txt*.

For security reasons, I have blurred the e-mail IDs.

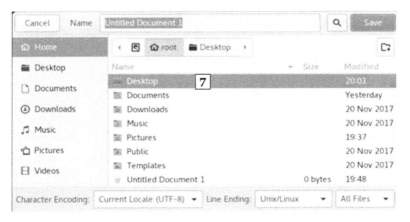

2.   To open the **Mass Mailer Attack** tool on Kali Linux, go to **Applications** > **Social Engineering Tools** > click on the **SET** icon, as shown in the following screenshot:

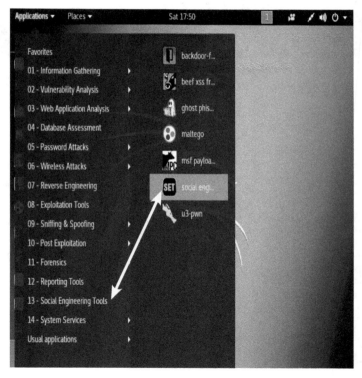

3.   **For first time users:** It will ask whether you agree with the terms of usage. Type *y* to agree to the terms and press *Enter* to open the SET. Type *1*and press *Enter* to open the **Social-Engineering Attacks** tools. Then, type '5' and press **Enter** to open the **Mass Mailer Attack** tool, as follows:

4. Now, type 2 and press *Enter* to open **E-mail attack Mass Mailer**.

Now, provide the path of e-mail list in this section **Path to the file to import into SET**. For this example, I use */root/Desktop/email-list.txt*

Then, type *1* and press *Enter* to select option **Use a gmail Account for your email attack**.

Further, type the following details in the next section:

Your gmail email address: Add your Gmail address here

The FROM Name the user will see: *COMPUTER SECURITY EXPERT*

Email password:

Flag this message/s as high priority? [yes | no]: *no*

Do you want to attach a file - [y/n]: *n*

Email subject: *NEED ANY SOLUTION REGARDING COMPUTER SECURITY?!*

Send the message as html or plain? 'h' or 'p' [p]: *p*

Enter the body of the message, type END (capitals) when

finished: *Please send me your detail information here. END*
Next line of the body: *Thanks*
Next line of the body: *END*

Website Attack Vector (site cloning)

In *Website Attack Vector* or *site cloning attack*, a website clone is created, which looks exactly same as the original website. The website is hosted on an external server. So, any http request sent to the server will display the cloned page. It is the most prominent way of phishing website attack for hacking a username and password.

Follow the steps:

1. To open the Website Attack Vector tool on Kali Linux, go to **Applications > Social Engineering Tools > SET.**

2. Type *1* and press *Enter* to open **Social-Engineering Attacks** tools. Then, type *2* and press *Enter* to open the **Website Attack Vector** tool, as follows:

```
                              Terminal                    ○  ⊙  ⊗
 File  Edit  View  Search  Terminal  Help
The Java Applet Attack method will spoof a Java Certificate and deliver ^
a metasploit based payload. Uses a customized java applet created by Tho
mas Werth to deliver the payload.

The Metasploit Browser Exploit method will utilize select Metasploit bro
wser exploits through an iframe and deliver a Metasploit payload.

The Credential Harvester method will utilize web cloning of a web- site
that has a username and password field and harvest all the information p
osted to the website.

The TabNabbing method will wait for a user to move to a different tab, t
hen refresh the page to something different.

The Web-Jacking Attack method was introduced by white_sheep, emgent. Thi
s method utilizes iframe replacements to make the highlighted URL link t
o appear legitimate however when clicked a window pops up then is replac
ed with the malicious link. You can edit the link replacement settings i
n the set_config if its too slow/fast.

The Multi-Attack method will add a combination of attacks through the we
b attack menu. For example you can utilize the Java Applet, Metasploit B
rowser, Credential Harvester/Tabnabbing all at once to see which is succ
essful.

The HTA Attack method will allow you to clone a site and perform powersh
ell injection through HTA files which can be used for Windows-based powe
rshell exploitation through the browser.

   1) Java Applet Attack Method
   2) Metasploit Browser Exploit Method
   3) Credential Harvester Attack Method
   4) Tabnabbing Attack Method
   5) Web Jacking Attack Method
   6) Multi-Attack Web Method
   7) Full Screen Attack Method
   8) HTA Attack Method

 99) Return to Main Menu

set:webattack>3
```

3. Now Type 3 and press *Enter* to open **Credential Harvester Attack Method**. As we need to clone the site, we need to enter 2 for **Site Cloner**.

```
                              Terminal                    ⊖  ⊕  ⊗
 File  Edit  View  Search  Terminal  Help
 The first method will allow SET to import a list of pre-defined web
 applications that it can utilize within the attack.

 The second method will completely clone a website of your choosing
 and allow you to utilize the attack vectors within the completely
 same web application you were attempting to clone.

 The third method allows you to import your own website, note that y
 ou
 should only have an index.html when using the import website
 functionality.

    1) Web Templates
    2) Site Cloner
    3) Custom Import

    99) Return to Webattack Menu

 set:webattack>2
 [-] Credential harvester will allow you to utilize the clone capabil
 ities within SET
 [-] to harvest credentials or parameters from a website as well as p
 lace them into a report
 [-] This option is used for what IP the server will POST to.
 [-] If you're using an external IP, use your external IP for this
 set:webattack> IP address for the POST back in Harvester/Tabnabbing
 [192.168.17.128]:
 [-] SET supports both HTTP and HTTPS
 [-] Example: http://www.thisisafakesite.com
 set:webattack> Enter the url to clone:www.facebook.com



 The best way to use this attack is if username and password form
 fields are available. Regardless, this captures all POSTs on a websi
 te.
 [*] The Social Engineer Toolkit Credential Harvester Attack
 [*] Credential Harvester is running on port 80
 [*] Information will be displayed to you as it arrives below:
 192.168.17.128 - - [20/Feb/2018 14:14:25] "GET / HTTP/1.1" 200 -
```

4.   Press *Enter* on **IP address for the POST back in Harvester/
     Tabnabbing [192.168.17.128]**. Here, I used *192.168.17.128* as
     the IP address.

5.   Enter the URL to clone, here I entered *www.facebook.com*

6.   After this, if a user wants to open *192.168.17.128* in a web
     browser in Kali Linux, it shows a clone of *Facebook login page*.
     Whenever the user enters the credentials (**User ID** or **Email
     ID** and **Password**) and **Log In**, the data is sent to your SET,
     and you will see the users credential displayed on your
     screen as follows:

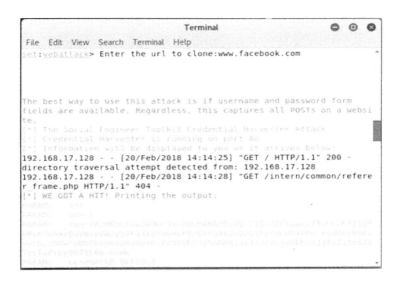

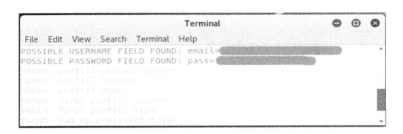

In the preceding screenshot, the **email** (e-mail ID) and **pass** (password) are hidden for security reasons.

 To maximize the chances of success for the attack, you can hide the real link with website services such as https://bitly.com/.

CHAPTER 7

Footprinting

Footprinting

Footprinting is defined as the process of gathering information of an organization's network and systems. It begins by determining the target system, application, or physical location of the target. Major possible information to be gathered about a target during footprinting by an attacker or hacker are domain name, specific IP addresses, system architecture, intrusion detection system, network blocks, network services and applications, access control mechanisms, authentication mechanisms, phone numbers, and contact addresses.

Techniques used for footprinting

Domain name information (DNS lookup)

You can use the following websites to get detailed information about a domain name information, including its owner, its registrar, date of registration, expiry, name server, owner's contact information, etc.

- *www.whois.com/whois*
- *www.who.is*
- *www.whois.domaintools.com*
- *www.ultratools.com/tools/dnsLookup*

Using www.whois.com/whois website to DNS lookup

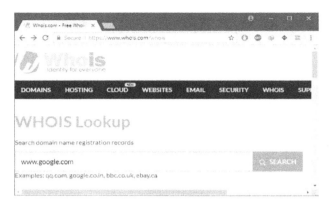

Enter the domain name and click on **SEARCH**. Here, I enter *www.google.com*. It will show you the domain information, registrant contact, administrative contact, technical contact, and raw whois data, as follows:

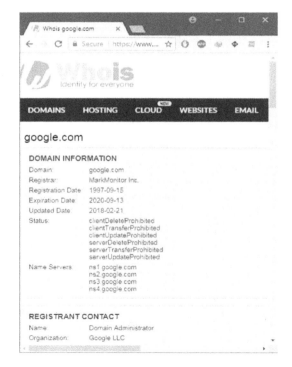

Finding the IP address and host provider

You can use the following websites to get detailed information about IP address, host provider, name servers, etc.

- *www.whoishostingthis.com*
- *www.webhostinghero.com/who-is-hosting*
- *www.hostingchecker.com*
- *www.ultratools.com/tools/ipWhoisLookup*
- *www.hostadvice.com/tools/whois*

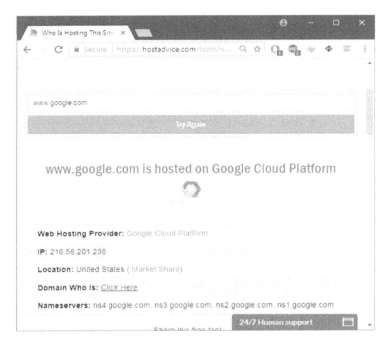

Finding an IP address location

Use the following websites to find an IP address location:*www.iplocation.net*

- *www.ip2location.com*
- *www.ipfingerprints.com*
- *www.whatismyipaddress.com/ip-lookup*
- *www.melissadata.com/lookups/iplocation.asp*

Traceroute

Traceroute is a network utility that records the route (the specific gateway computers at each hop) through the Internet between your computer and a specified destination computer network. It also calculates and displays the amount of time each hop took.

In Windows, the command used for Traceroute is *tracert*. It is often used with other networking-related Command Prompt commands such as *ping*, *ipconfig*, *netstat*, *nslookup*, and others.

Using the tracert command in Windows

1. Press the Windows key + *R*, type *cmd* and press *Enter* to open the **Command Prompt** window:

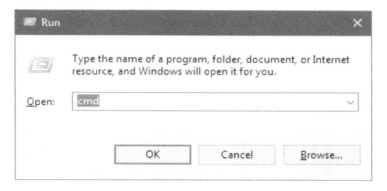

2. Then, type *tracert* and domain name or IP address. Here, I entered *tracert www.google.com:*

```
C:\Windows\system32\cmd.exe                                    —    □    ×
C:\Users\SRB>tracert www.google.com

Tracing route to www.google.com [172.217.163.132]
over a maximum of 30 hops:

  1     1 ms    <1 ms    <1 ms  192.168.1.1
  2    11 ms    13 ms    12 ms  103.193.56.1
  3    53 ms   239 ms    17 ms  218.248.171.54
  4    35 ms    34 ms    35 ms  218.248.235.162
  5    34 ms    36 ms    34 ms  72.14.195.21
  6    35 ms    34 ms    33 ms  74.125.242.145
  7    35 ms    34 ms    34 ms  216.239.42.245
  8    35 ms    34 ms    34 ms  maa05s04-in-f4.1e100.net [172.217.163.132]

Trace complete.

C:\Users\SRB>
```

Using the traceroute command in Kali Linux

1. Open the Terminal window.

2. Type the following command and press *Enter*.

   traceroute domain name or IP address

   Example: *traceroute www.facebook.com*:

Gaining the archive of a targeted website (history of the website)

Wayback Machine (www.archive.org/web) is a digital archive of the World Wide Web and other information on the Internet created by the Internet Archive.

Using Wayback Machine

1. Go to the website *www.archive.org/web*.

2. Now, enter the targeted website and click on **BROWSE HISTORY**. Here, I entered *www.msn.com*.

3. Then, you can choose the year and date to archive the targeted website, as shown in the following screenshot:

DMitry – information gathering tool on Kali Linux

DMitry (Deepmagic Information Gathering Tool) is a UNIX/ (GNU) Linux command-line application coded in C. It has the ability to gather as much information as possible about a host. It is used to gather possible subdomains, e-mail addresses, uptime information, TCP port scan, whois lookups, and more.

To know more about Dmitry on Kali Linux, open the Terminal, enter *dmitry* and press *Enter*, as shown in the following screenshot:

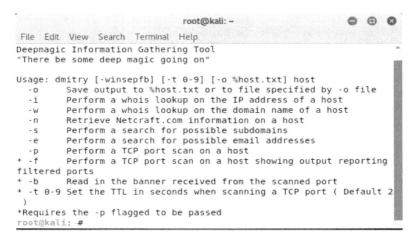

Some common code used in *DMitry* are as follows:

Code	Working
dmitry -i host	Perform a whois lookup on the IP address of a host
dmitry -w host	Perform a whois lookup on the domain name of a host
dmitry -n host	Retrieve Netcraft.com information on a host
dmitry -s host	Perform a search for possible subdomains
dmitry -e host	Perform a search for possible e-mail addresses
dmitry -p host	Perform a TCP port scan on a host
In the Host *field, you need to enter the targeted website or IP address*	

Web spiders (or Web crawler)

A Web spider is a program that visits websites and reads their pages and other information in order to create entries for a search engine index. It is also known as a Web crawler. *Googlebot, Yahoo Slurp,* and *MSNbot* are the major web crawler programs that harvest information for search engines.

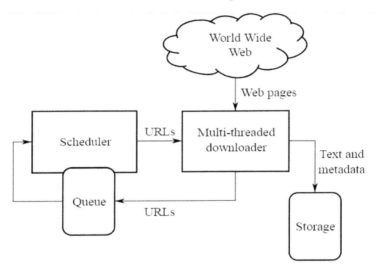

CHAPTER 8

Scanning

Scanning

After the phase of footprinting (reconnaissance and information gathering), scanning is performed. Scanning is an important phase, and a hacker needs to have knowledge of operating systems, ports, protocols, and networks. In this phase, the target system is scanned to look for open ports and vulnerabilities.

Types of scanning

There are three types of scanning process: port scanning, network scanning, and vulnerability scanning.

Port scanning

Port scanning refers to the observation of computer ports in order to locate holes within the specific computer ports.

The ports numbers can be in these three ranges: well-known ports from 0 to 1023, registered ports from 1024 to 49151, and dynamic ports from 49152 to 65535.

Some common port numbers are mentioned in the following table:

Service	Port number
FTP	20 and 21
TELNET	23
SMTP	25
HTTP	80
HTTPS	443
POP3	110
DNS	53

Network scanning

The network scanning process identifies the active hosts on a network, either to attack them or as a network security assessment. Network hosts are identified by their individual IP addresses. The purposes of network scanning are

- **R**ecognize available UDP and TCP network services running on the targeted hostsRecognize filtering systems between the user and the targeted hosts

- Determine the operating systems (OSs) in use by assessing IP responsesEvaluate the target host's TCP sequence number predictability to determine sequence prediction attack and TCP spoofing.

Vulnerability scanning

The vulnerability scanning process first identifies the OS and version number, including service packs that may be installed. Then, it detects specific weak spots in an application software or the OS, which could be used to crash the system or compromise it for undesired purposes.

Using of scanning tools

Nmap - Network Mapper in Windows

Nmap is a security scanner used to discover hosts and services on a computer network. Nmap can be downloaded from the following link:

www.nmap.org/download.html

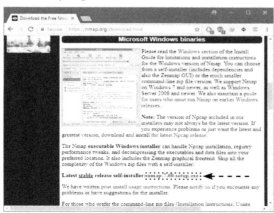

It is available for Windows GUI (Zenmap) and CLI (nmap). After the installation, Open the **Nmap - Zenmap GUI** icon from Desktop.

You can perform the following types of scanning by using this tool:*Intense scan* performs TCP port scanning along with detection of OS.

- *Intense scan plus UDP* performs intense scanning of UDP ports.

- *Intense scan, all TCP* ports scans all available 65535 ports.

- *Intense scan, no ping* option excludes pinging the target from the intense scan.

- *Ping scan* only performs ping the target.

- *Quick scan* performs quick intense scan by limiting the number of TCP ports (100 most common TCP ports).

- *Quick scan plus* performs quick scan along with OS detection.

- *Quick traceroute* shows the targeted packet route.

- *Regular scan* performs pinging and scanning of 1,000 default TCP ports.

Nmap - Network Mapper in Kali Linux

Nmap for Linux RPM source and binaries: *https://nmap.org/download.html*

Nmap package for Kali Linux: *git://git.kali.org/packages/nmap.git*

Tool*	Description	Use this code on Kali Linux to know more
nping	Network packet generation tool / ping utility	*nping –h*
ndiff	Utility to compare the results of Nmap scans	*ndiff -h*
ncat	Concatenate and redirect sockets	*ncat –h*
nmap	The network mapper	*nmap –h*
Tools included in the nmap package		

nmap usage on Kali Linux

Scan in verbose mode (-*v*), enable OS detection, version detection, script scanning, and traceroute (-*A*), with version detection (-*sV*) against the target IP (*192.168.1.100*)

Open the Terminal and enter this code on Kali Linux : *nmap -v -A -sV 192.168.1.100*

```
                          root@kali: ~                    ⊖  ⊡  ⊗
 File  Edit  View  Search  Terminal  Help
root@kali:~# nmap -v -A -sV 192.168.1.100

Starting Nmap 7.60 ( https://nmap.org ) at 2018-02-26 12:12 EST
NSE: Loaded 146 scripts for scanning.
NSE: Script Pre-scanning.
Initiating NSE at 12:12
Completed NSE at 12:12, 0.00s elapsed
Initiating NSE at 12:12
Completed NSE at 12:12, 0.00s elapsed
Initiating Ping Scan at 12:12
Scanning 192.168.1.100 [4 ports]
Completed Ping Scan at 12:12, 0.04s elapsed (1 total hosts)
Initiating Parallel DNS resolution of 1 host. at 12:12
Completed Parallel DNS resolution of 1 host. at 12:12, 0.09s ela
psed
Initiating SYN Stealth Scan at 12:12
Scanning 192.168.1.100 [1000 ports]
Discovered open port 110/tcp on 192.168.1.100
Discovered open port 139/tcp on 192.168.1.100
Discovered open port 135/tcp on 192.168.1.100
Discovered open port 445/tcp on 192.168.1.100
Discovered open port 443/tcp on 192.168.1.100
```

nping usage on Kali Linux

Using TCP mode (*--tcp*) to probe port 22 (*-p 22*) using the SYN flag (*--flags syn*) with a TTL of 2 (*--ttl 2*) on the remote host (*192.168.1.100*)

Open the Terminal and enter this code in Kali Linux: *nping --tcp -p 22 --flags syn --ttl 2 192.168.1.100*

```
                            root@kali: ~                    ●  ▣  ✖

 File  Edit  View  Search  Terminal  Help
root@kali:~# nping --tcp -p 22 --flags syn --ttl 2 192.168.1.100

Starting Nping 0.7.60 ( https://nmap.org/nping ) at 2018-02-26 12
:15 EST
SENT (0.0550s) TCP 192.168.17.128:6706 > 192.168.1.100:22 S ttl=2
 id=40024 iplen=40  seq=1515139327 win=1480
SENT (1.0561s) TCP 192.168.17.128:6706 > 192.168.1.100:22 S ttl=2
 id=40024 iplen=40  seq=1515139327 win=1480
RCVD (1.0593s) TCP 192.168.1.100:22 > 192.168.17.128:6706 RA ttl=
128 id=62413 iplen=40  seq=1875799164 win=64240
SENT (2.0591s) TCP 192.168.17.128:6706 > 192.168.1.100:22 S ttl=2
 id=40024 iplen=40  seq=1515139327 win=1480
RCVD (3.0609s) TCP 192.168.1.100:22 > 192.168.17.128:6706 RA ttl=
128 id=62414 iplen=40  seq=1950684190 win=64240
SENT (3.0609s) TCP 192.168.17.128:6706 > 192.168.1.100:22 S ttl=2
 id=40024 iplen=40  seq=1515139327 win=1480
RCVD (4.0623s) TCP 192.168.1.100:22 > 192.168.17.128:6706 RA ttl=
128 id=62415 iplen=40  seq=1021927346 win=64240
SENT (4.0623s) TCP 192.168.17.128:6706 > 192.168.1.100:22 S ttl=2
 id=40024 iplen=40  seq=1515139327 win=1480

Max rtt: 1001.652ms | Min rtt: 2.908ms | Avg rtt: 668.551ms
Raw packets sent: 5 (200B) | Rcvd: 3 (138B) | Lost: 2 (40.00%)
Nping done: 1 IP address pinged in 5.10 seconds
root@kali:~#
```

Scanning for specific port or port range

If you are looking for a specific port or a port range, Nmap uses the *-p* switch to designate a port or port range. Here, I am looking for a port range of 25-150.

Open the Terminal and enter this code in Kali Linux: *nmap 192.168.1.100 –p25-150*

```
                          root@kali: ~              ⊖  ▣  ✕

  File   Edit   View   Search   Terminal   Help
  root@kali:~# nmap 192.168.1.100 -p25-150

  Starting Nmap 7.60 ( https://nmap.org ) at 2018
  -02-26 12:32 EST
  Nmap scan report for 192.168.1.100
  Host is up (1.0s latency).
  Not shown: 123 closed ports
  PORT      STATE SERVICE
  110/tcp open  pop3
  135/tcp open  msrpc
  139/tcp open  netbios-ssn

  Nmap done: 1 IP address (1 host up) scanned in
  2.39 seconds
  root@kali:~# █
```

NOTE Some common tools for perform scanning are Angry IP scanner, SolarWinds Engineer Ping Sweep, OpenVAS, NetScan Tool, Wireshark, Nessus, OpenSSH, etc.

Hiding your IP address or how to stay anonymous online

There are many possible methods to stay anonymous online. Some of them are described as follows.

Hiding your IP address with a virtual private network (VPN)

Hiding your IP address with a **virtual private network** (VPN) offers a connectivity to another network, and when connected, your computer receives a new IP address from a VPN provider. Some major VPN providers are Hide My Ass, Vypr VPN, Express VPN, Pure VPN, etc.

Masking your IP address with proxies

A proxy server (sometimes called an "open proxy" or just "proxies") can be used to re-route your browser (Chrome, Firefox, Safari, Internet Explorer, or Edge) around company or school content filters. Major proxy list websites are:*www.free-proxy-list.net*

- *www.spys.one/en*
- *www.hidemy.name/en/proxy-list*

Using the Tor Browser

The Tor Browser is a free Web browser that conceals your IP address every time you go online anonymously.

Using free/public Wi-Fi or someone else's network

You can use public free Wi-Fi of other networks to temporarily hide your usual IP address.

CHAPTER 9

Cryptography

Cryptography

In cryptography, *crypt* means secret or hidden and *graphy* means writing. So, literally, cryptography means secret or hidden writing. Cryptography is the process of converting recognizable data into an encrypted code for transmitting it over a network (either trusted or untrusted). Data is encrypted at the source, that is sender's end, and decrypted at the destination, that is receiver's end. Generally, *cryptography* is the study of encryption and decryption algorithms. The mathematical formula used to encrypt the code is known as the encryption algorithm.

 Plaintext and ciphertext
Cryptography is most often associated with scrambling plaintext (readable and understandable data, sometimes referred to as cleartext) into ciphertext (a process called encryption), then back again (known as decryption). Ciphertext should be unreadable and show no repeatable pattern to ensure the confidentiality of the data.

The three elements to data security and encryption are described as follows:

- *Confidentiality* ensures that no one can read the message except the intended receiver.

- *Integrity* assures the receiver that the received message has not been altered in any way from the original.

- The *authentication* process provides one's identity.

Confidentiality, integrity, and authentication are known as the CIA triad.

* *Non-repudiation* is a mechanism to prove that the sender really sent this message.

Types of cryptography

Generally, cryptography is classified into three categories as follows:

- **Secret key cryptography (SKC)**
- **Public key cryptography (PKC)**
- **Hash functions**

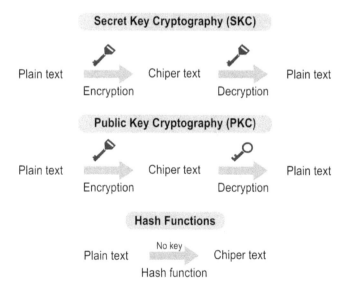

SKC

The SKC method uses a single key for both encryption and decryption. The sender uses the key to encrypt the plaintext and sends the ciphertext to the receiver. The receiver applies the same key to decrypt the message and recover the plaintext. Because a single key is used for both functions, SKC is also called *symmetric encryption* or *symmetric cryptography*.

Some major SKC algorithms are described as follows:

- **Data Encryption Standard** (**DES**) is a block cipher employing a 56-bit key that operates on 64-bit blocks. DES uses a key of only 56 bits, and thus, it is now susceptible to "brute force" attacks. It was one of the oldest encryption schemes developed by IBM.

 Triple-strength DES (3DES) applies the DES algorithm three times (hence, the name "triple DES"), making it slightly more secure than DES.

- **Advanced Encryption Standard (AES)** can use a variable block length and key length; the latest specification allowed any combination of keys lengths of 128, 192, or 256 bits and blocks of length 128, 192, or 256 bits. It was developed by the **National Institute of Standards and Technology** (**NIST**).

- **International Data Encryption Algorithm** (**IDEA**) is written by Xuejia Lai and James Massey, in 1992, Ascom. It is a 64-bit SKC block cipher using a 128-bit key.

- **Rivest Cipher 2** (**RC2**) is a 64-bit block cipher using variable-sized keys designed to replace DES.

- **Rivest Cipher 4** (**RC4**) is a stream cipher using variable-sized keys. It is widely used in commercial cryptography products and can only be exported using keys that are 40 bits or less in length. It is developed by Ronald Rivest of RSA fame. It is used in VoIP and WEP.

 Rivest Ciphers (*aka* Ron's Code): Named for Ron Rivest, a series of SKC algorithms.

- **Blowfish** is a 64-bit block cipher invented by Bruce Schneier. It can be optimized for 32-bit processors with large data caches; it is significantly faster than DES. Its key lengths can vary from 32 to 448 bits in length.

> **NOTE** Twofish is a stronger version of Blowfish using a 128-, 192- or 256-bit key. It is designed to be highly secure and highly flexible, well suited for large microprocessors, 8-bit smart card microprocessors, and dedicated hardware.

PKC

PKC uses two related keys known as a key pair. A public key is made available to anyone who might want to send you an encrypted message. A second, private key is kept secret, so that only you know it. It is also known as *asymmetric encryption* or *asymmetric cryptography*.

Asymmetric cryptography is slower than symmetric cryptography. It is not used for bulk or streaming encryption due to its speed limitations.

Some common PKC algorithms are described as follows:

- **Rivest–Shamir–Adleman** (**RSA**) is of the most popular encryption algorithm, invented in 1977 by three MIT scientists (Ronald *Rivest [R]*, Adi *Shamir [S]*, and Leonard *Adleman [A]*). It uses factorization of very large prime numbers as the relationship between the two keys.

- **Public Key Infrastructure** (**PKI**) is a combination of policies, procedures and technology needed to manage digital certificates in a PKC scheme. The purpose of PKI is to make sure that the certificate can be trusted.

Hash functions

Hash functions, also called *message digests* or *one-way encryption*, are algorithms that use no key. Instead, a fixed-length hash value is computed based upon the plaintext that makes it impossible for either the contents or length of the plaintext to be recovered. Hash functions are also commonly employed by many operating systems to encrypt passwords.

Some well-known hash function algorithms are described as follows:

- **Message digest** (**MD**) algorithms are a series of byte-oriented algorithms that produce a 128-bit hash value from an arbitrary-length message. *MD2* is designed for systems with limited memory, such as smart cards. *MD4* is designed specifically for fast processing in software. *MD5* is slower because more manipulation is made to the original data. It accepts variable length message from the user and converts it into a fixed 128-bit message digest value.

- **Secure Hash Algorithm (SHA)** is used to generate condensed representation of a message. SHA-0 produces 120-bit hash value. SHA-1 produces 160-bit hash value. SHA-2 has two hash functions, such as SHA-256 and SHA-512, and can use 32-bit and 64-bit words, respectively. SHA-3 (aka Keccak) can support hash output sizes of 256 and 512 bits.

- **HAsh of VAriable Length (HAVAL)** has many levels of security. It can create hash values that are 128, 160, 192, 224, or 256 bits in length.

- *Whirlpool* is developed by V. Rijmen and P.S.L.M. Barreto. It operates on messages less than 2^{256} bits in length and produces a message digest of 512 bits.

- *Tiger* is developed by Ross Anderson and Eli Biham. It is designed to be secure, run efficiently on 64-bit processors. Tiger/192 produces a 192-bit output and is compatible with 64-bit architectures; Tiger/128 and Tiger/160 produce the first 128 and 160 bits, respectively, to provide compatibility with the other hash functions.

Online encryption and decryption

Website	Encryption and decryption types
http://md5decrypt.net/en	MD5, MD4 SHA1, SHA256, SHA384, SHA512, XOR, Morse code, Gronsfeld cipher, Tritheme cipher, ROT13, Caesar cipher, Polybius square, Vigenere cipher, letters frequency
www.freeformatter.com/cryptography-and-security.html	MD2, MD4, MD5, SHA1, SHA-224, SHA-256, SHA-384, SHA-512, RIPEMD128, RIPEMD160, RIPEMD320, Tiger, Whirlpool, GOST3411, **hash-based message authentication code (HMAC)**
https://hash.online-convert.com	Adler32, Blowfish, CRC-32, CRC-32B, DES, GOST, Haval-128, MD4, MD5, SHA1, SHA-224, SHA-256, SHA-384, SHA-512, Tiger128, Tiger160, Tiger192, Whirlpool

Block cipher versus stream cipher

Comparison	Block cipher	Stream cipher
Converting method	Converts the plaintext by taking its block at a time	Converts the text by taking one byte of the plaintext at a time
Complexity level	Simple	Complex
Number of bits used	64 bits or more	8 bits
Algorithm modes used	ECB (electronic code book) CBC (cipher block chaining)	CFB (cipher feedback) OFB (output feedback)
Reversibility	Hard	Easy by using XOR
Example	*Feistel* cipher	*Vernam* cipher

Cryptanalysis

Cryptanalysis is the investigation of cryptosystems, ciphertext, and ciphers in order to reveal the hidden meaning or details of the system itself.

Cryptanalysis techniques and attacks

Cryptanalysis techniques and attacks are methods of evading the security of a cryptographic system by finding weaknesses in the cipher, protocol, or key management.

Some major cryptanalysis techniques and attacks are as follows:

- *Ciphertext–only attack* requires the attacker to obtain several messages encrypted using the same encryption algorithm. The two key indicators of this attack are: (i) the attacker does not have the associated plaintext and (ii) the attacker attempts to crack the code by looking for patterns and using statistical analysis.

- *Known–plaintext attack* requires the attacker to have the plaintext and ciphertext of one or more messages. The goal of this attack is to discover the key. This attack can be used if the attacker knows a portion of the plaintext of a message.

- *Chosen–plaintext attack* is applied when the attacker either knows the encryption algorithm or has access to the device used to do the encryption. The attacker can encrypt the chosen plaintext with the targeted algorithm to derive information about the key.

- *Chosen–ciphertext attack* is applied when the attacker knows the decryption algorithm. The attacker can decrypt the chosen chipper text with the targeted algorithm to derive information about the key.

- *Brute force attack* involves trying every possible combination of characters or data in order to find the key in order to decrypt an encrypted message.

- *Dictionary attack* involves trying by guess at the key of a ciphertext by attempting many different common passwords and possible passwords that are likely to be used by humans. A dictionary attack makes use of what is called a dictionary, which stores common English words, phrases, and passwords ready to guess as the key.

BitLocker drive encryption

BitLocker drive encryption is an encryption tool used for Windows 10 Pro and Windows 10 Enterprise. Follow the steps to turn on BitLocker drive encryption on the operating system drive:

1. Go to **Control Panel** > **System and Security** > **BitLocker Drive Encryption.**

2. Under **BitLocker Drive Encryption**, click on **Turn on BitLocker**:

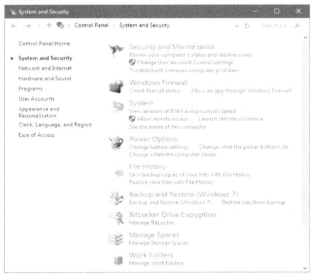

NOTE If you get the following error, then try the following method:

Turn on BitLocker without TPM

i.   Use the Windows key + *R* keyboard shortcut to open the *Run* command, type *gpedit.msc*, and click on **OK**.

ii. Under **Computer Configuration**, expand **Administrative Templates > Windows Components > BitLocker Drive Encryption > Operating System Drives:**

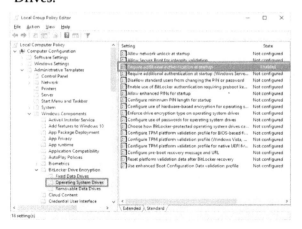

iii. On the right side, double-click on **Require additional authentication at startup**.

iv. Select **Enabled**.

v. Make sure to check the **Allow BitLocker without a compatible TPM (requires a password or a startup key on a USB flash drive)** option:

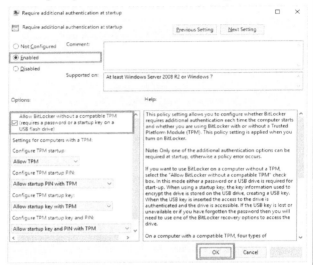

vi. Click on **OK** to complete this process.

3. Choose how you want to unlock your drive during startup: **Insert a USB flash drive** or **Enter a password**. Here, I selected **Enter a password** to continue.

4. Enter a password that you'll use every time you boot Windows 10 to unlock the drive, and click on **Next** to continue. (Make sure to create a strong password mixing uppercase, lowercase, numbers, and symbols.)

5. You will be given the choices to save a recovery key to regain access to your files in case you forget your password. Options include:

   • **Save to your Microsoft account**

   • **Save to a USB flash drive**

   • **Save to a file**

   • **Print the recovery**

Select the option that is most convenient for you, and save the recovery key in a safe place. I selected **Save to a file** and click on **Next** to continue.

6. Select the encryption option that best suits your scenario:

    - **Encrypt used disk space only (faster and best for new PCs and drives)**

    - **Encrypt entire drive (slower but best for PCs and drives already in use)**

    I selected **Encrypt entire drive (slower but best for PCs and drives already in use)** and click on **Next** to continue.

7. Choose between the two encryption options:
    - **New encryption mode (best for fixed drives on this device)**

    - **Compatible mode (best for drives that can be moved from this device)**

    I selected **New encryption mode (best for fixed drives on this device)** and click on **Next** to continue.

8. Check the **Run BitLocker system** check option, and click on **Continue**.

9. Finally, restart your computer to begin the encryption process.

10. On reboot, BitLocker will prompt you to enter your encryption password to unlock the drive. Type the password and press *Enter*.

NOTE *Some other encryptions tools are as follows*

Whole disk encryption tool: DiskCryptor, FileVault, The Linux Unified Key Setup

Shredding tool: Eraser, Darik's Boot and Nuke

File encryption tool: AES Crypt, Challenger

Portable drive encryption tool: BitLocker To Go, SecurStick

Data in transit encryption tool: OpenSSL, Stunnel

Remote management encryption tool: OpenSSH, PuTTY, PowerShell

CHAPTER 10

Stenography

Stenography

The word steganography comes from the Greek *steganos*, meaning covered or secret, and *graphy*, meaning writing or drawing. It is the process of hiding data in other types of data such as images or text files.

Steganography process

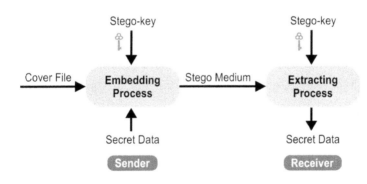

Steganalysis is the process of detecting hidden information inside a file.

Carrier or cover file is an original message or a file in which hidden information will be stored inside of it.

Stego-key is the special key used in both embedding and extracting process.

Embedding process is the process of embedding the secret data into cover file by using a Stego-key.

Extracting process is the process of extracting the cover file to gain secret data by using a Stego-key.

Stego-medium is the medium in which the information is hidden.

Embedded or payload or secret data is the information that is to be hidden or concealed.

> **NOTE** *Watermarking* is used for the protection of the documents by keeping a copyright of the owner. It is basically used for multimedia files to protect intellectual property rights.

Steganography methods

Steganography methods are differentiated on the basis of the media in which we hide the data. These are *text, image, audio, video*, and *executable*.

Text steganography

The text steganography method hides the text behind some other text file. Some major text steganography techniques are as follows:

- **Selective hiding**: This method hides the characters in the first (or any specific location) characters of the words. Concatenating those characters help extracting the text. But, this technique requires huge amount of plaintext.

- **HTML web page steganography**: This method hides text using the fact that attributes of HTML tags are case insensitive. Those characters can then be used to retrieve the original text.

- **Word shifting**: This method uses shifting words horizontally, and by changing distance between words, information is hidden in the text. This method is acceptable for texts where the distance between words is varying. This method can be identified less, because change of distance between words to fill a line is quite common.

- **Line shifting**: This method uses the lines of the text that are vertically shifted to some degree (for example, each line is shifted 1/300 inch up or down), and information is hidden by creating a unique shape of the text.

- **Character sequences**: This method hides information within character sequences is character-based information that is available and transmitted over networks. One approach to text steganography might hide information in what appears to be a random sequence of characters.

- **Word sequences**: This method is used to solve the problem of detection of non-lexical sequences, actual dictionary items by encoding one or more bits of information per word.

- **Syntactic method**: This method is applied by placing some punctuation marks, such as full stop (.) and comma (,) in proper places; one can hide information in a text file. This method requires identifying proper places for putting punctuation marks.

- **Semantic method**: This method uses the synonym of certain words, thereby hiding information in the text. The synonym substitution may represent a single- or multiple-bit combination for the secret information.

Audio steganography

Audio steganography uses digital sound to hide secret data. This method embeds the secret message in WAV, AU, MP3, etc. sound files. Some audio steganography techniques are as follows:

- **Low-bit encoding**: This is used when pitch period prediction is conducted during low-bit speech encoding, thereby maintaining synchronization between information hiding and speech encoding.

- **Phase encoding**: This uses stream file splits audio into blocks and embeds whole secret sequence into phase spectrum of the first block.

- **Direct-sequence spread spectrum** (**DSSS**): This spreads steganography by multiplying it by certain pseudorandom sequence. In this technology, a data signal at the sending station is combined with a high data rate bit sequence, which divides user data based on a spreading ratio.

Video steganography

Video steganography uses digital videos or video streams to hide secret data. This method embeds the secret message in AVI, WMV, MP4, 3GP, etc. videos files. Digital videos and video streams are transmitted more and more frequently on Internet websites, such as Facebook and YouTube, imposing a larger practical significance on video steganography.

> *Real-time video steganography* considers each frame that is shown by the machine at any moment, irrespective of whether it is photo, text, or anything else, as an image. Then, the system divides the image into small blocks. If the pixel colors of the blocks are similar, it changes the color characteristics of a number of these pixels to a certain extent, so data information is hidden in the image.

Image steganography

Images are the most popular cover objects used for steganography. Image steganography uses digital images to hide secret data.

An image is a collection of pixels containing different light intensities in different areas of the image. Depending on the type of message and type of the image, different algorithms are used.

Least significant bit (LSB) insertion is a well-known algorithm for image steganography; it involves the modification of the LSB layer of image. In this technique, the message is stored in the LSB of the pixels, which could be considered as random noise. Thus, altering them does not have any obvious effect on the image. LSB modification technique for images holds good if any kind of compression is done on the resultant stego-image, such as JPEG, GIF. JPEG images use the discrete cosine transform to achieve compression.

Masking and filtering works better on 24-bit and gray-scale images. This method hides information in a way similar to watermarks on actual paper and is sometimes used as a digital watermark. To ensure that changes cannot be detected, make the changes in multiple small proportions.

Adaptive steganography method is a special case of two methods: spatial domain and transform domain. It is also known as "Statistics Aware Embedding" and "Masking". Global features of images are used before embedding secret data in coefficients of discrete cosine transform (DCT) or discrete wavelet transform (DWT).

Discrete cosine transformation (DCT) converts the uncompressed image into JPEG compressed type. It is based on data hiding used in the JPEG compression algorithm to transform successive 8 × 8 pixel blocks of the image from spatial domain to 64 DCT coefficients each in frequency domain.

Discrete wavelet transformation (**DWT**) splits the signal into set of basic functions. There are two types of wavelet transformations: one is *continuous* and other is *discrete*. This is the new idea in the application of wavelets; in this, the information is stored in the wavelet coefficients of an image, instead of changing bits of the actual pixels. It also performs local analysis and multi-resolution analysis.

Executable file steganography

The executable file steganography method hides executable files (.exe files) within the image File (.jpeg, .png, etc.).

Steganography in Windows

Hide data file in image in Windows

1. Gather the file you wish to bind, and the image file, and place them in a folder. I will be using *C:\New Folder*:

Image file in the example: *image.jpg*

Data file in the example: *data.txt*

In the data file, you can insert your secret message.

2. Add the file/files you will be injecting into the image into a WinRAR (.rar or .zip). From here on, this will be referred to as *data.rar*, as follows:

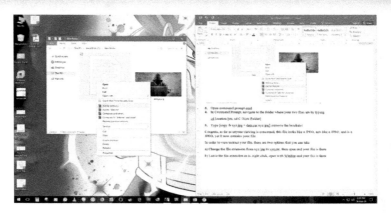

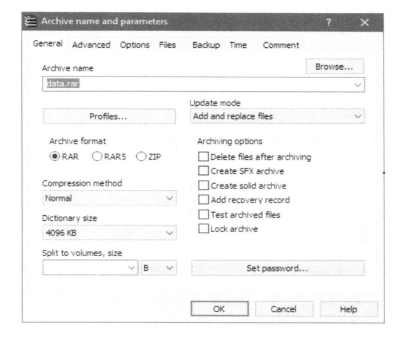

3. Open Command Prompt by using Windows + *R* and type *cmd*; press *Enter*.

4. In Command Prompt, navigate to the folder where your two files are, by typing
   cd location [ex: cd C:\New Folder]

5.   Type *copy /b image.jpg + data.rar newimage.jpg*:

Congrats, as far as anyone viewing is concerned, this file looks like a JPEG, acts like a JPEG, and is a JPEG, yet it now contains your file.

In order to view/extract your file, right-click on *newimage.jpg* open with WinRAR and your file is there.

Steganography in Kali Linux

Steghide

Steghide is a steganography program that can hide data in various kinds of image files and audio files. Major features of steghide are as follows:

- Compression of embedded data
- Encryption of embedded data
- Embedding of a checksum to verify the integrity of the extracted data
- Support for JPEG, BMP, WAV, and AU files

Installing steghide

To install *steghide*, open the Terminal and type *apt-get install steghide* and press *Enter*; then, enter *Y* to continue the installation, as in the following screenshot:

```
                              root@kali: ~                    ⊖  ▣  ✕
 File  Edit  View  Search  Terminal  Help
root@kali:~# apt-get install steghide
Reading package lists... Done
Building dependency tree
Reading state information... Done
The following additional packages will be installed:
  libmcrypt4 libmhash2
Suggested packages:
  libmcrypt-dev mcrypt
The following NEW packages will be installed:
  libmcrypt4 libmhash2 steghide
0 upgraded, 3 newly installed, 0 to remove and 0 not upgraded.
Need to get 302 kB of archives.
After this operation, 881 kB of additional disk space will be used.
Do you want to continue? [Y/n] Y█
```

Hide text file in image using steghide

6. Create a folder (named as *steghide*) in in root home folder and place the image file (named as *picture.jpg*) and text message file (named as *secret.txt*) there:

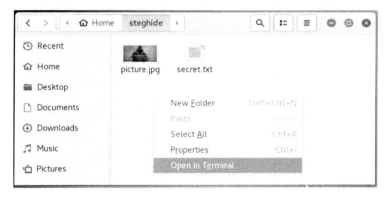

7.   Now, right-click on the white space in the *steghide* folder and click on **Open in Terminal**.

8.   Now, enter the code *steghide embed -cf picture.jpg -ef secret.txt* and press *Enter*. Then, enter and re-enter the passphrase. This command will embed the file *secret.txt* in the cover file *picture.jpg*:

```
                        root@kali: ~/steghide                    ⊖  ⊡  ⊗
File  Edit  View  Search  Terminal  Help
root@kali:~/steghide# steghide embed -cf picture.jpg -ef secret.txt
Enter passphrase:
Re-Enter passphrase:
embedding "secret.txt" in "picture.jpg"... done
root@kali:~/steghide#
```

Extracting text file from image using steghide

After you have embedded your secret data, as shown earlier, you can send the file *picture.jpg* to the person who should receive the secret message. The receiver has to use steghide in the following way:

1. Create a folder (named as *steghide*) in in root home folder and place the received image file (named as *picture.jpg*) there:

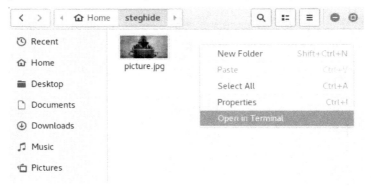

2. Now, right-click on the white space in *steghide* folder and click on **Open in Terminal**.

3. Now, enter the code *steghide extract -sf picture.jpg* and press *Enter*.

4. If the supplied passphrase is correct, the contents of the original file *secret.txt* will be extracted from the stego file *picture.jpg* and saved in the current directory, as shown in the following screenshot:

Stegosuite

Stegosuite is a graphical user interface (GUI) with similar functionality as steghide.

Installation of stegosuite

To install *stegosuite*, open the Terminal and type *apt-get install stegosuite* and press *Enter*; then, enter *Y* to continue the installation, as shown in the next screenshot:

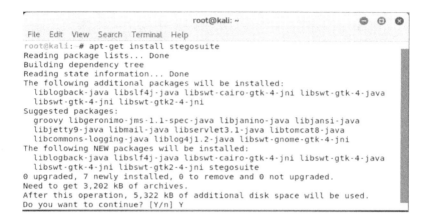

Embed text file in image using stegosuite

1. You need to run it from the **Application** menu (or you can just search it).

2. Go to **File > Open** and open the image you want to use. Right-click on the **File** section and select **Add files** and select your *secret.txt* file.

3. Type in a passphrase and click on **Embed**. Few seconds and it will create a new file *picture_embed.jpg*.

Extracting text file from image using stegosuite

If you want to extract a text file or data from the image, simply open the image, type in the passphrase and click on **Extract**.

Online steganography tool

Some online websites to encode text into image and decode image into text are as follows:

- *www.incoherency.co.uk/image-steganography*
- *www.futureboy.us/stegano*
- *http://stylesuxx.github.io/steganography/*

 Some commonly used steganography tools are OpenStego, QuickStego, Xiao Steganography, Steghide, and Imagesteganography.

CHAPTER 11

System Hacking

System Hacking

System hacking performs the following actions:

- Cracking passwords.
- Executing applications.
- Understand keyloggers and spyware.
- Understand rootkits.
- Hiding files and folder.
- Clearing the tracks.

Password and its types

Password is a string of characters that allows access to a computer, interface, or system.

Types of passwords

Type	Example
Only letters	password
Only numbers	1234567
Only special characters	***@@@
Letters and numbers	password007
Only letters and special characters	*password*
Only numbers and special characters	***007
Letters, numbers, and special characters	*@007password

NOTE   A *strong password* is a combination of letters (both uppercase and lowercase), numbers, and special characters, for example, 365max*@HACK.

Password cracking techniques

Password cracking is the process of attempting to gain unauthorized access to restricted systems by obtaining the correct password (or recover passwords from systems). A hacker may use different types of attacks to get the password. Types of password cracking attacks are *active online attacks, passive online attacks, offline attacks* and *non-electronic attacks.*

Active online attacks

In an active online attack, the attacker performs password cracking by directly communicating with the victim machine. An active online attack can performed by dictionary attack, hybrid attack, brute force attack, and spyware/keyloggers attack.

Dictionary attack attempts to use passwords from a list of dictionary words.

Hybrid attack attempts with dictionary file, and it substitutes various numbers and symbols for characters in the password.

Brute Force attack tries every combination of characters until the password is broken.

Spyware/keylogger attack performs an attack by installing spyware and keylogger into a victim's system to collect login credentials (username and password). Spyware and keylogger run in the background and send back all credentials to the attacker.

Passive online attacks

In a passive online attack, the attacker performs password cracking without communicating with the authorizing party. A passive online attack can performed by wire sniffing, **man-in-the-middle** (**MITM**), and replay attack.

Wire sniffing is performed by running packet sniffer tools on the local area network (LAN) to access and record the raw network traffic. The captured data may include passwords that can be used to gain unauthorized access to the target system.

MITM is applied by gaining access to the communication channels between the victim and server; then, it captures passwords in the process.

Replay attack occurs when packets and authentication tokens are captured using a sniffer. After the relevant information (such as password) is extracted, the tokens are placed back on the network to gain access.

Offline attacks

In an offline attack, the attacker copies the target's password file and then tries to crack passwords in his own system at different location. An offline attack can performed by rainbow table attack and distributed network attack.

Rainbow table attack uses pre-computed hashes. A rainbow table is a precomputed table that contains word lists like dictionary files and brute force lists and their hash value.

Distributed network attack (**DNA**) technique is used for recovering passwords from hashes or password-protected files using the unexploited processing power of machines across the network to decrypt passwords. A DNA Manager coordinates the attack and allocates small portions of the key search, and a DNA Client runs in the background, consuming only unused processor time to crack the password.

Non-electronic attacks

In non-electronic attacks, the attacker cracks the password by using non-technical skills. Non-electronic attacks can performed by social engineering, dumpster diving, shoulder surfing, and guessing. For more details, please refer *Human-based social engineering* in *Chapter 6, Social Engineering and Reverse Social Engineering*.

Default passwords

A default password is a password supplied by the manufacturer with new equipment (e.g., switches, hubs, routers) that is password protected. Attackers can use default passwords in the list of words or dictionary that they use to perform a password guessing attack.

There are some websites that contain the database of default usernames, passwords, ports, and other networking information. Some major websites that contain default password database are as follows:

- *www.defaultpassword.com*
- *www.cirt.net/passwords*
- *www.routerpasswords.com*

Password cracking tools

Tools	Features	Website for download
Cain and Abel	It is a password recovery tool for Microsoft Windows and used for a dictionary attack, brute-force and cryptanalysis attack, network password sniffer.	www.oxid.it/cain.html
John the Ripper	It is primarily used to crack UNIX passwords but also available for Linux, Mac, and Windows. It supports brute force password cracking, dictionary attacks.	www.openwall.com/john
OphCrack	It is a rainbow-table based tool for password cracking on Windows. It can also be used on Linux or Mac. It can crack LM and NTLM hashes.	www.ophcrack.sourceforge.net
RainbowCrack	It uses rainbow tables to crack hashes; in other words, we can say it uses process of a large-scale time-memory trade for effective and fast password cracking. It is available for Windows and Linux.	www.project-rainbowcrack.com
THC Hydra	It is a network password cracking tool available for Windows, Linux, and Mac. It uses network to crack remote systems passwords.	www.thc.org/thc-hydra
Aircrack-NG	It is used for cracking of Wi-Fi passwords that can crack WPA or WEP passwords. The FMS attack is utilized with other useful attacking methods for cracking of passwords. It is available on Linux and Windows systems.	www.aircrack-ng.org

Cracking password by using of Cain and Abel

Before opening Cain and Abel, you must turn off Windows firewall or any other firewall (antivirus firewall).

Go to **Control Panel** > **System and Security** > **Windows Firewall**:

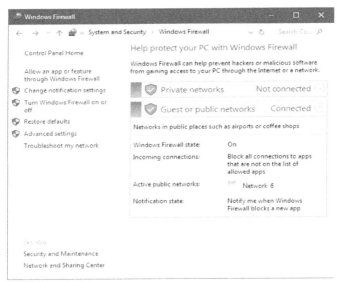

Then, click on **Turn of Windows Firewall (not recommended)**:

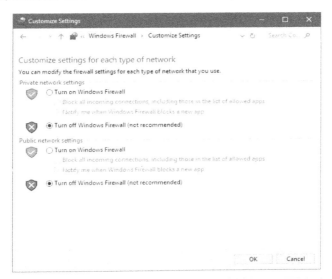

Click on **Turn off Windows Firewall (not recommended)** under both private and public network setting, as seen in the preceding screenshot.

Turn off the firewall of your antivirus or Internet security (if any):

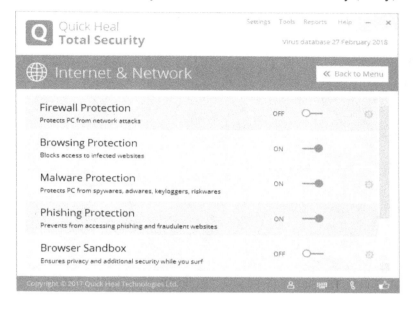

To open Cain and Abel, right click on the **Cain** icon and click on **Run as administrator**:

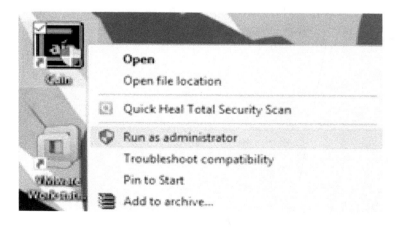

Click on **Cracker** and then the **Add to list** ✚ icon, then click on **Next**. Then, the following will be seen:

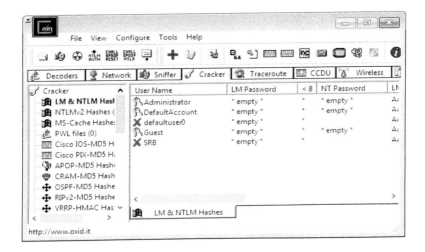

Right-click on the username (which you want to crack the password), then navigate to Brute-Force Attack > **NTML Hashes**:

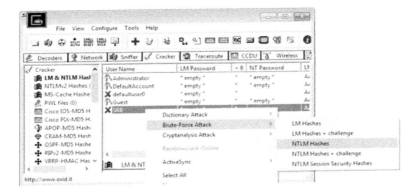

Then, select **Predefined** as per your need and click on **Start** to crack the password:

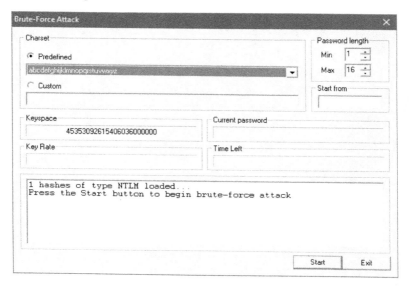

After some time, it will show you the password as follows:

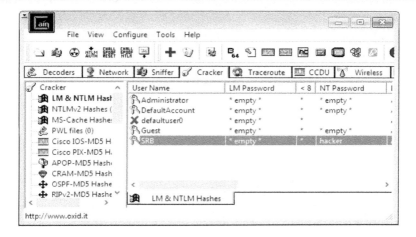

Keyloggers

Keyloggers are referred as remote access software that can allow access to locally recorded data from a remote location. This communication can happen by using one of the following methods: (i) uploading the data to a website, database, or an FTP server, (ii) periodically e-mailing data to a predefined e-mail address, (iii) wirelessly transmitting data through an attached hardware system, and (iv) software enabling remote login to your local machine.

Additional features of some keyloggers are clipboard logging, screen logging, control text capture, activity tracking, and recording of search engine queries.

 Some major keylogger tools are Free Keylogger, REFOG Free Keylogger, Real Keylogger, Revealer Keylogger, etc.

Spyware

Spyware is a program or software that is embedded on a computer and records passwords, Internet browsing, cookies, and can sometimes control computers services and remotely execute commands. Spyware applications are typically bundled as a hidden component of freeware or shareware programs that can be downloaded from the Internet.

Some major spyware threats are CoolWebSearch (CWS), Gator (GAIN), Internet Optimizer, BlazeFind, Hot as Hell, Transponder (vx2), etc.

Some major spyware removal tools are SUPERAntiSpyware, Malwarebytes, SpywareBlaster, Avast, AVG, Spybot - Search & Destroy, etc.

Rootkits

Rootkit is a stealth type of malware that is designed to hide the existence of certain programs on computer system from regular detection methods as to allow it or another malicious process privileged access to computer system. It works using a simple concept called modification. In general, software is designed to make specific decisions based on very specific data. A rootkit locates and modifies the software so that it makes incorrect decisions.

There are basically three different types of rootkits.

- *Kernel rootkits* usually add their own code to parts of the operating system core.

- *User-mode rootkits* are especially targeted to Windows to start up normally during the system start up, or injected into the system by a so-called dropper.

- *MBR rootkits* or *bootkits* (*bootkit = rootkit + boot capability*) cannot be detected by standard means of an operating system because all their components reside outside of the standard filesystems.

Hiding files and folders

Hiding files and folders on a system can performed by a hacker or attacker to prevent their detection. These files may then be used to launch an attack on the system.

Hiding files and folders in Windows using File Explorer

1. Go to the location where the file or folder is located.

2. Right-click on the file or folder (which you want to hide), then click on **Properties**:

3. Then, click on (put a check mark) the **Hidden** and click on **OK**. Again click on **A**pply changes to this folder, subfolder and files. Click on **OK**:

After completing the steps, the items with the hidden attribute will no longer be visible.

To make it visible again, open **File Explorer**, go to **View** and click on (or put a tick mark) **Hidden items**:

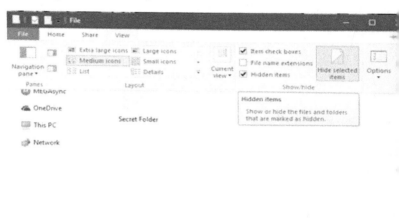

Hiding files and folders in Windows using the Command Prompt

1. Open **Start**. Do a search for **Command Prompt** and click on the result:

2. So, my file location is **Desktop** > **File**.Type *cd Desktop* and press *Enter*.

    Type *cd File* and press *Enter*:

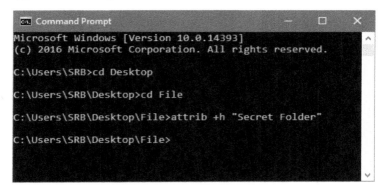

3. Then, to hide **Secret Folder**, type *attrib +h "Secret Folder"* and press *Enter*. Quotation marks are only necessary when there are spaces in the name. After completing the steps, the items with the hidden attribute will no longer be visible.

Making hidden files and folders visible again, use this code after to navigate to the hidden items location: *attrib -h "Secret Folder"*

Clearing the tracks

A hacker removes the identity or activities evidence on the system to prevent tracing of their identity or location by authorities by clearing audit policy the event log.

Clearing the audit policy

1.   Open the **Command Prompt** (**Run as administrator**):

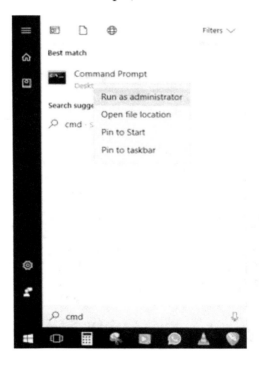

2. To clear audit policy, type this code *auditpol.exe/clear* and press *Enter*. Then, type *Y* and press *Enter*:

Clearing even log

1. Go to **Control Panel** > **System and Security** > **Administrative Tools**, open **Event Viewer**.

2. Go to **Windows Logs** > **Application**, select the information files that you want to clear, then click on **Clear Log ...** on the **Actions** panel (right-side panel). Then, click on **Save and Clear**. You can use same process to clear events on *Security, Setup, System* and *Forwarded Events*:

CHAPTER 12

Malware

Malware

Malware is short for *malicious software*, meaning software that can cripple or disrupt the system's operation, allowing attacker access to confidential and sensitive information, as well as the ability to spy on personal and private computers.

Some major types of malwares are described as follows.

Virus

VIRUS is short for **Vital Information Resources Under Siege**. It is a contagious program or code that attaches itself to another piece of software, and then reproduces itself when that software is run. Most often, this is spread by sharing software or files between computers.

Types of virus

Major types of virus are: **Boot sector virus:** It infects the master boot record of the hard disk. The virus either copies the master boot program to another part of the hard disk or overwrites it.

Examples: Polyboot.B, AntiEXE, Disk Killer, Michelangelo, etc.

- **Program virus:** It infects executable program files, such as those with extensions like .BIN, .COM, .EXE, .OVL, .DRV (driver), and .SYS (device driver). It is loaded in memory during execution, taking the virus with them. It becomes active in memory, making copies of itself and infecting files on disk.

  Examples: Sunday, Cascade

- **Multipartite virus:** It is a hybrid of boot and program virus. It infects program files, and when the infected program is executed, it infects the boot record. When you boot the computer next time, the virus from the boot record loads in memory and then starts infecting other program files on disk.

  Examples: Ghostball, Invader, Flip, etc.

- **Stealth virus:** It has the ability to avoid detection. It may either redirect the disk head to read another sector instead of the one in which it resides or it may alter the reading of the infected file's size shown in the directory listing.

  Examples: Frodo, Joshi, Whale

- **Polymorphic virus:** It can encrypt its code in different ways so that it appears differently in each infection.

  Examples: Stimulate, Cascade, Phoenix, Evil, Proud, Virus 101

- **Macro virus:** It infects files that are created using certain applications or programs (such as MS Word, MS Excel, etc.) that contain macros. It causes a sequence of actions to be performed automatically when the application is started or something else triggers it. It is often spread as an e-mail virus.

  Examples: Melissa.A., Relax, Bablas, etc.

- **Resident virus:** It resides in the RAM. From there, it can overcome and interrupt all of the operations executed by the system, such as corrupting files and programs that are opened, closed, copied, renamed, etc.

  Examples: Randex, CMJ, Meve, etc.

- **Direct action virus:** It is considered to be "non-resident" and functions by selecting one or more files to infect each time the infected program is executed. It infects those whose directories are attached with the AUTOEXEC.bat file path.

  Example: Vienna

- **Overwrite virus:** It deletes the information contained in the files that it infects, execute it partially or totally useless once it has been infected.

  Examples: Trj.Reboot, Trivial.88.D., Way, etc.

- **Web scripting virus:** It allows the attackers to inject client-side scripting into the web page. It can bypass access controls, steal user information from a web browser.

  Example: JS Fortnight

- **FAT virus:** It can be especially dangerous, by preventing access to certain sections of the disk where important files are stored. It can cause information loss from individual files or even entire directories.

   Examples: Link virus

Some well-known viruses are:

Year	Virus name
1971	Creeper
1982	Elk Cloner
1988	The Morris Internet worm
1999	Melissa
2000	ILoveYou
2001	Code Red and Nimda
2003	SQL Slammer & Blaster
2004	Sasser and Mydoom
2008	Conficker
2010	Stuxnet and Zeus
2011	Flashback
2014	CryptoLocker
2016	Mirai
2017	WannaCry

Worm

A worm replicates without targeting and infecting specific files that are already present on a computer. It can destroy the files and data in it. Basically, whereas viruses add themselves inside existing files, worms carry themselves in their own containers. Worms generally use a computer network to spread, relying on security failures on the target computer in order to access it, and delete data.

Examples: Melissa, Morris, Mydoom, Sasser, Blaster, etc.

Trojan horse

Trojan horse, commonly known as a "Trojan," is a type of malware that disguises itself as a normal file or program to trick users into downloading and installing malware. It is actually the non-self-replicating malware. It can give a malicious party remote access to an infected computer. Once an attacker has access to an infected computer, it is possible for the attacker to steal data (logins, financial data, and even electronic money), install more malware, modify files, monitor user activity (screen watching, keylogging, etc.), use the computer in botnets, and anonymize Internet activity by the attacker.

Examples: NetBus, Beast, Blackhole exploit kit, Tiny Banker Trojan, Clickbot. A, Zeus, etc.

Trojans ride on the backs of other programs and are usually installed on a system without the user's knowledge. A Trojan can be sent to a victim system in many ways, such as an **instant messenger** (**IM**) attachment, IRC, an e-mail attachment, NetBIOS file sharing, a downloaded Internet program, etc.

Overt and covert channel

An *overt channel* is the normal and legitimate way that programs communicate within a computer system or network. A *covert channel* uses programs or communications paths in ways that were not intended. Trojans can use covert channels to communicate and to send instructions to the server component on the compromised system.

Some common Trojans and their default port numbers are as follows:

Trojan	Protocol	Port
Deep Throat	UDP	2140 and 3150
BackOrifice	UDP	31337 or 31338
Master's Paradise	TCP	3129, 40421, 40422, 40423, and 40426

NetBus	TCP	12345 and 12346
Whack-a-mole	TCP	12361 and 12362
NetBus 2	TCP	20034
GirlFriend	TCP	21544

Types of Trojans are summarized as follows:

Trojans	Use
Remote Access Trojans (RATs)	Gain remote access to a system
Proxy Trojans	Tunnel traffic or launch hacking attacks via other systems
FTP Trojans	Create an FTP server in order to copy files onto a system
Security Software Disabler Trojans	Stop an antivirus software
Data-sending Trojans	Find data on a system and deliver data to a hacker
Destructive Trojans	Delete or corrupt files on a system
Denial-of-service Trojans	Launch a denial-of-service attack

Backdoor

A backdoor is a set of programs that a hacker installs on a target system to allow access to the system at a later time. A backdoor can be embedded in a malicious Trojan. The main objective of installing a backdoor on a system is to give hackers access into the system at a time of their choice. The key is that the hacker knows how to get into the backdoor undetected and is able to use

it to hack the system further and look for important information. A backdoor is also known as a *trapdoor* or *manhole*.

RAT

RAT is a class of backdoors used to enable remote control over a compromised machine. It provides apparently useful functions to the user, and at the same time, open a network port on the victim computer. Once the RAT is started, it behaves as an executable file, interacting with certain registry keys responsible for starting processes and sometimes creating its own system services. RATs hook themselves into the victim operating system and always come packaged with two files: the *client file* and the *server file*. Unlike viruses and worms, RATs can exist well before detection and even remain after removal. They operate in a stealth mode and are usually rather small so as to avoid detection.

RATs are commercially available, such as Poison Ivy, Dark Comet, Blackshades, and can be maliciously installed on endpoints using drive-by-download and spear-phishing tactics.

Rootkit

Rootkit is a collection of software specifically designed to permit malware that gathers information, into your system. These software work like a back door for malware to enter and wreak havoc, and are now being used extensively by hackers to infect systems. A rootkit installation can either be automatic or an attacker can install it once they have obtained administrator privileges.

Examples: NTRootkit, Sony BMG copy protection rootkit, etc.

Ransomware

Ransomware blocks access to the data of a victim, threating to either publish it or delete it until a ransom is paid. Worse yet, there is no guarantee that paying a ransom will return access to the data or prevent it from deletion. This type of malware basically infects the system from the inside, locking the computer and making it useless.

Examples: Reveton, CryptoLocker, CryptoWall, WannaCry, etc.

Keylogger

A keylogger records all the information that is typed using a keyboard. It is not capable of recording information that is entered using virtual keyboards and other input devices. It can store the gathered information and send it to the attacker, who can then extract sensitive information such as username and passwords, as well as personal and bank details. Some common keylogger software are Actual Keylogger, REFOG Keylogger, DanuSoft Keylogger, BlackBox Express, etc.

Adware

Adware stands for advertising-supported software is a type of malware that automatically delivers advertisements. Common examples of adware include pop-up ads on websites and advertisements that are displayed by software. Often times, software and applications offer "free" versions that come bundled with adware. Most adware is sponsored or authored by advertisers and serves as a revenue-generating tool. While some adware is solely designed to deliver advertisements, it is not uncommon for adware to come bundled with spyware that is capable of tracking user activity and stealing information.

Spyware

Spyware is a type of malware that functions by spying on user activity without their knowledge. It spies on users activity monitoring, collecting keystrokes, data harvesting (account information, logins, financial data), and more. It often has additional capabilities as well, ranging from modifying security settings of software or browsers to interfering with network connections. It spreads by exploiting software vulnerabilities, bundling itself with legitimate software, or in Trojans.

Spam

Most spams are commercial advertisements that are sent as an unwanted e-mail to users. Spams are also known as electronic junk mails or junk newsgroup postings. Spamming is a method of flooding the Internet with copies of the same message.

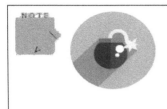

NOTE *Logic bomb* is a piece of malicious code inserted into computer system or software application that implements a malicious function after specific conditions are met. When it implements malicious attack after a specific date/time interval, then it is called time *bomb*.

Techniques of malware attacks

Some common techniques of malware attacks are as follows:

- **Hacking:** It is an attempt to exploit a computer system or a private network inside a computer. It is the process to gain an unauthorized access to control over computer network security systems for some illicit purpose.

- **Cracking:** It is the act of breaking into a computer system. A cracker can be doing this for profit, maliciously, for some altruistic purpose or cause.

- **Spoofing:** It occurs when cybercriminals try to get into your computer by masquerading as a trusted source. Examples include e-mail spoofing, IP spoofing, and address bar spoofing.

- **Phishing:** It occurs when cybercriminals try to get sensitive information from you, such as credit card numbers and passwords. Some specific techniques include spear phishing (target-specific people or departments), whale phishing (targets important people such as CEOs), and SMiShing (phishing via text messages), and vishing (voice phishing that takes place over the phone, usually through impersonation).

- **Pharming:** It occurs when a malicious website that resembles a legitimate website is used to gather usernames and passwords.
- **Salami technique:** It is a type of computer fraud in which small amounts of money are transferred from numerous customer accounts into an account held under a false name.

Symptoms of malware attacks

While types of malware differ greatly in how they spread and infect computers, they all can produce similar symptoms. Computers that are infected with malware can exhibit any of the following symptoms:

- Increased CPU usage
- Slow computer or web browser speeds
- Problems connecting to networks
- Freezing or crashing
- Modified or deleted files
- Appearance of strange files, programs, or desktop icons
- Programs running, turning off, or reconfiguring themselves (malware will often reconfigure or turn off antivirus and firewall programs)
- Strange computer behavior
- E-mails /messages being sent automatically and without an user's knowledge (a friend receives a strange e-mail from you that you did not send)

Some common terms related to malware are as follows:

Botnet: A number of Internet-connected devices that are running one or more bots. Botnets are used to perform distributed denial-of-service attacks, send spam, and steal data.

Containment: The process of stopping the spread of malware and preventing further damage to hosts.

Eavesdropping: It is the unauthorized interception of a private digital communication.

Endpoint: A security approach to the protection of computer networks that are remotely bridged to client devices. Devices that are not in compliance can thereby be provisioned with limited access.

Payload: The part of the malware program that actually does the damage.

Threat: In computing security, a computer or network is deemed under threat when it harbors persistent software vulnerabilities, thereby increasing the possibility or certainty of a malicious attack.

Track: Evidence of an intrusion into a system or a network. Advanced malware can clean folders, clear event logs, and hide network traffic to cover their tracks.

Zombie: A computer connected to the Internet that has been compromised by a hacker, computer virus, or Trojan horse. It can be used to perform malicious tasks.

CHAPTER 13

Sniffing Packet, Packet Analyzer and Session Hijacking

Sniffing

Sniffing (packet sniffing) is the process of monitoring and capturing all the network packets passing through a given network using sniffing tools (sniffer). It is a form of phone tapping and get to know about the conversation. It is sometime referred as **wiretapping**.

An attacker can sniff many sensitive information from a network, such as DNS traffic, e-mail traffic, web browsing traffic, chat sessions, FTP passwords, telnet passwords, and router configuration.

Packet analyzer

A packet analyzer is used to capture and record network traffic that passes over a digital network. It analyzes network traffic and generates a customized report to assist organizations in managing their networks. It can be used by hackers to intrude on networks and steal information from network transmissions. It is also known as a *sniffer, network analyzer*, or *protocol analyzer*.

Types of sniffing

Generally, sniffing are of two types, such as *active sniffing* and *passive sniffing*.

Active sniffing

Active sniffing is performed on a switched network. It depends on injecting packets into the network that causes traffic. It is required to bypass the segmentation that switches provide. A switch maintains its own ARP cache-keeping track of which host is connected to which port. The Address Resolution Protocol (ARP) resolves IP addresses to the MAC address of the interface to send data inside network.

Switched Ethernet does not broadcast all information to all systems on the LAN. The switch regulates the flow of data between its ports by actively monitoring the MAC address on each port, which helps it pass data only to its intended target.

Some of the active sniffing methods are ARP spoofing, MAC flooding, MAC duplicating, DNS poisoning, etc.

Passive sniffing

Passive sniffing is performed on a hub. On a hub device, the traffic is sent to all the ports. In a network that uses hubs to connect systems, all hosts on the network can see the traffic. So, an attacker can easily capture traffic going through. Most modern networks use switches. Therefore, passive sniffing is less effective than active sniffing.

Some major sniffing tools

Sniffing tools	Website for download
Cain and Abel	*www.oxid.it/cain.html*
Wireshark	*www.wireshark.org*
Ettercap	*www.ettercap-project.org*
Kismet	*www.kismetwireless.net*
Tcpdump	*www.tcpdump.org*
Dsniff	*www.monkey.org/~dugsong/dsniff*

Sniffing passwords on LAN using Cain and Abel

Please turn off the Windows firewall or any other third-party firewall so that all the packets are captured efficiently.

1. Open the Cain and Abel tool (Run as administrator).

2. Go to the Sniffer Tab and click on Configure in the main menu to configure your packet listening adapter.

3. Select the appropriate network adapter for your network that you want to sniff the packets for plaintext passwords. And, click on OK:

4. Click on the green adapter icon as shown in the following screenshot. This means that you just configured the adapter and now you are turning it on:

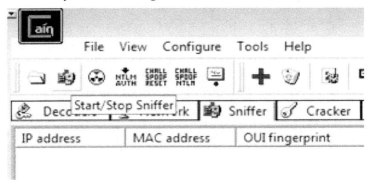

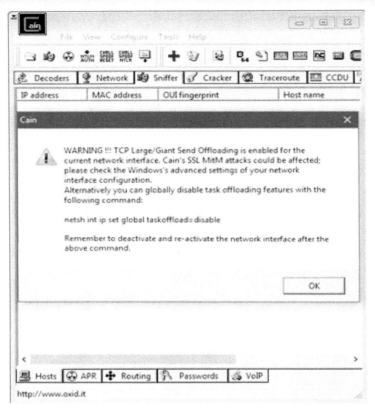

5. Now, select the APR tab below as shown, and now, first click on the right-side upper pane area. When you click on that area the blue plus (+) icon will get enabled. Press that blue plus (+) icon.

6. We need to select the router's IP address and click on OK. This means that we want to listen to every packet that is sent to the router. If we select any other IP address in our LAN network, then we can listen to only that particular host on the network. As the router responds to all the request of hosts connected to a LAN. Thus, we can listen to all the hosts.

7. Now, click on the yellow circle icon as shown. This means that we are starting ARP poisoning:

8. We can see that, in the upper-right panel, there is an IP address of our router, and when we press that yellow circle icon (button), it performs ARP poisoning.

9. Next, click on the Password tab, which is at the bottom. We can see that we are getting passwords of HTTP, that is, plaintext session in our LAN network.

Using Wireshark

Download Wireshark from www.wireshark.org. After downloading, install it on to your computer system.
Capture data packets

Open Wireshark from Desktop or Start menu.

You can capture data packets by double-clicking on the name of a network interface under Capture. For example, if you want to capture traffic on your Wi-Fi, click on Wi-Fi, as shown in the following screenshot:

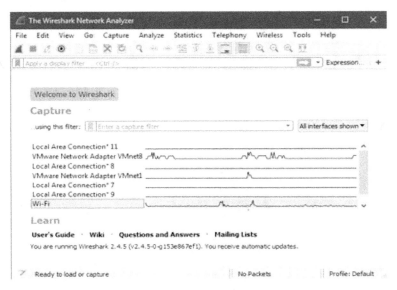

Then, you'll view the packets starting to appear in real time, as the next screenshot. Wireshark captures each packet sent to or from your system:

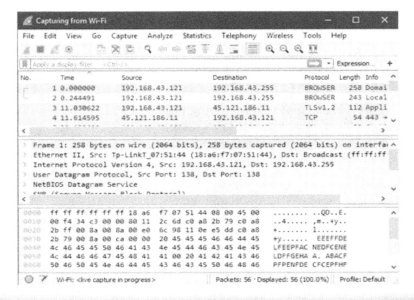

Click on the **Stop** button (red square button) near the top-left corner of the window when you want to stop capturing traffic:

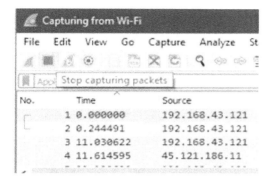

Color coding

To view color coding, click **View** > **Coloring Rules**. You can also customize and modify the coloring rules from here, if you like:

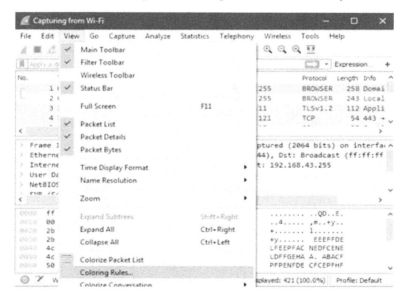

Save your own captures

You can save your own captures in Wireshark and open them later. Navigate to **File** > Save to save your captured packets.

Wireshark filters

To apply a filter, we have to type the name into the filter box at the top of the window, and then click on **Apply** (or press *Enter*). For example, type *dns* and you'll view only *DNS packets*.

When you start typing, Wireshark will help you autocomplete your filter:

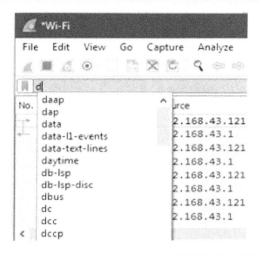

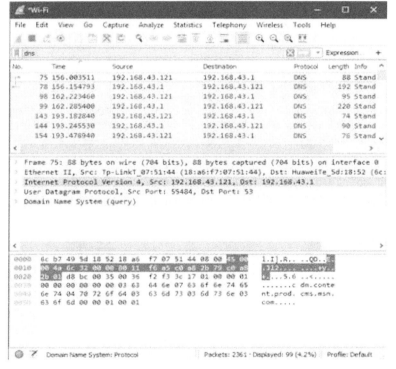

To analyze filters, go to **Analyze > Display Filters** to choose a filter from among the default filters included in Wireshark. From here, you can add your own custom filters and save them to easily access them in the future:

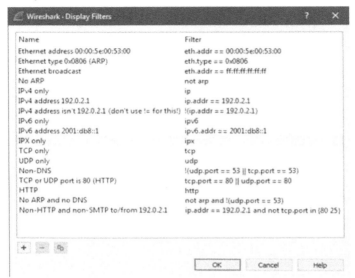

Session hijacking

Session hijacking (or *TCP session hijacking*), is performed by taking over a Web user session by covertly obtaining the session ID and masquerading as the authorized user. Once the user's session ID has been accessed (through session prediction), the attacker can masquerade as that user and do anything the user is authorized to do on the network. The session ID is normally stored within a cookie or URL. So, it is sometimes called as *cookie hijacking*. **Hamster** is the most used session hijacking tool in Kali Linux.

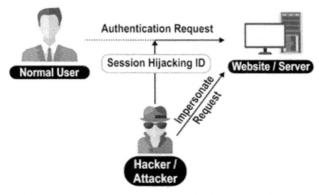

Session hijacking involves the following three steps to perpetuate an attack:

1. **Tracking the session:** In this step, the hacker identifies an open session and predicts the sequence number of the next packet.

2. **Desynchronizing the connection:** In this step, the hacker sends the valid user's system a TCP reset (RST) or finish (FIN) packet to cause them to close their session.

3. **Injecting the attacker's packet:** In this step, the hacker sends the server a TCP packet with the predicted sequence number, and the server accepts it as the valid user's next packet.

Types of session hijacking

There are two types of session hijacking: active and passive.

Active session hijacking

Active session hijacking is performed by finding an active session and taking over the session by using tools that predict the next sequence number used in the TCP session.

Passive session hijacking

Passive session hijacking performed by capturing a session and then watching and recording all the traffic that is being sent by the legitimate user. It is basically no more than sniffing. It gathers information such as passwords and then uses that information to authenticate as a separate session.

Session hijacking techniques

Session hijacking can be performed in a variety of techniques. The major ones include the following:

- **Session sniffing:** This involves the use of packet sniffing to read network traffic between two parties and eventually capture a valid **session ID** (**SID**).

- **Cross-site scripting (XSS):** This involves malicious payloads to trick the victim's browser into executing dangerous commands, eventually leading to the cookie theft.

- **Predictable session token:** This involves predicting the SID values that permit an attacker to bypass the authentication schema of an application.

- **Man-in-the-middle attack (MITM):** This is basically the interception of the TCP connection between the server and the client.

- **Man-in-the-browser attack:** This is similar to MITM attacks, but here the malicious attackers use Trojans to perform the interception and manipulation.

Session hijacking using Ettercap, Hamster, and Ferret (in Kali Linux)

1. Go to Applications > 09 - Sniffing & Spoofing > ettercap-graphical:

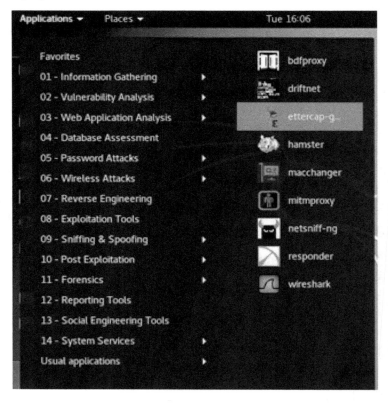

2.   Click on **Sniff**. Select the **Unified sniffing** option:

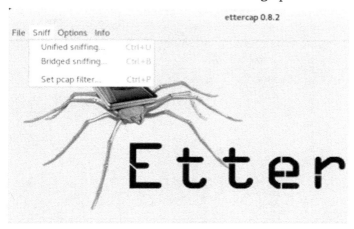

3.   It will ask for **Network Interface**. Select **eth0** and click on **OK**:

4.   Now, select **Hosts** and click on **Scan for Hosts** or press *Ctrl + S*. Now, go to **Hosts > Host List**.

5.   . It will show the IP addresses in the network. Select the target IP address (here I select **192.168.17.2**) and click on **Add to Target 1**:

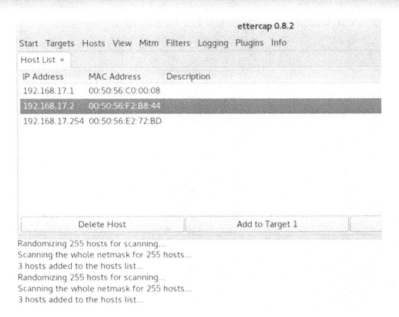

6. Now, select the **Mitm** option. Click on **ARP Poisoning**.

7. It will ask for sniff remote connections or only poison one-way. Check the **Sniff remote connections** option:

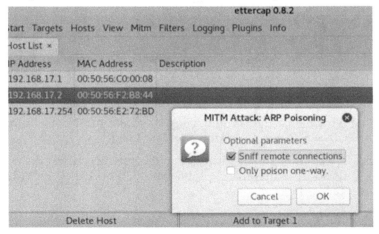

8. 8. Now, select the **Start** option and click on **Start sniffing** or press *Shift + Ctrl + W*. It will show sniffing.

9. Now open the **Hamster** tool (go to **Applications** > **09 - Sniffing & Spoofing** > **hamster**) to manipulate data by using a proxy:

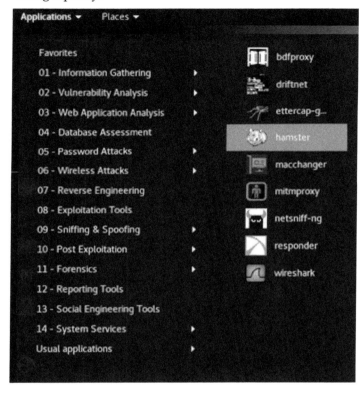

10. It will show the browser proxy such as *http://127.0.0.1:1234:*

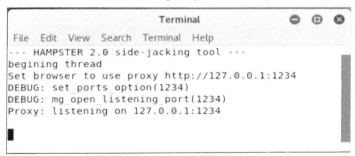

11. Now, open the **ferret** tool (go to **Applications** > **09 - Sniffing & Spoofing > ferret**) to grab the session cookies.

12. Type the command *ferret −i eth0*.

13. Now type *127.0.0.1:1234* in the browser and click on the target IP. It will show session cookies:

CHAPTER 14

Denial-of-Service Attack

Denial-o-service attack

A denial-of-service (DoS) attack is meant to shut down a computer system or network, making it inaccessible to its intended users. It can be performed by flooding the target with traffic or sending it information that triggers a crash.

> **NOTE** Some major DoS attack tools are PyLoris, **LOIC (low-orbit ion canon)**, Slowloris, QSlowloris, Tor's Hammer, etc.

Distributed DoS attack

A **Distributed DoS (DDoS)** attack can be performed by compromising multiple computer systems to attack a target, such as a server, website, or other network resource, and cause inaccessible service for users of the targeted resource.

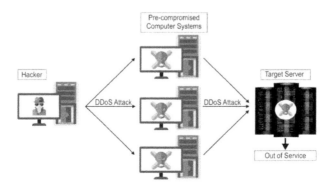

NOTE Some major DDoS attack tools are **high-orbit ion cannon (HOIC)**, hping, **R U Dead Yet? (R.U.D.Y.)**, DAVOSET, DDOSIM, etc.

Types of DoS and DDoS attacks

Generally, DoS and DDoS attacks can be divided into three types:

- **Volume-based attacks**: These include UDP floods, ICMP floods, and other spoofed-packet floods. The attack's goal is to saturate the bandwidth of the attacked site, and the magnitude is measured in **bits per second** (**Bps**).

- **Protocol attacks**: These include SYN floods, fragmented packet attacks, Ping of Death, Smurf DDoS, and more. This type of attack consumes actual server resources, or those of intermediate communication equipment, such as firewalls and load balancers, and is measured in **packets per second** (**Pps**).

- **Application layer attacks**: These include low-and-slow attacks; GET/POST floods; attacks that target Apache, Windows, or OpenBSD vulnerabilities; and more. Comprised of seemingly legitimate and innocent requests, the goal of these attacks is to crash the web server, and the magnitude is measured in **requests per second** (**Rps**).

Major DoS and DDoS attack techniques are as follows.

UDP flood

A UDP flood attack is performed by flooding a target with **User Datagram Protocol** (**UDP**) packets. The goal of the attack is to flood random ports on a remote host. This causes the host to repeatedly check for the application listening at that port, and (when no application is found) reply with an ICMP "Destination Unreachable" packet. This process vitalities host resources, which can ultimately lead to inaccessibility.

ICMP (Ping) flood

ICMP flood routs the target resource with the **Internet Control Message Protocol** (**ICMP**) echo request (ping) packets, generally sending packets without waiting for replies. The attack consumes the resources and available bandwidth, exhausting the network until it goes offline.

SYN flood

A SYN flood DDoS attack exploits a known weakness in the TCP connection sequence (the "three-way handshake") and sends a request to connect to a server, but never completes the handshake.

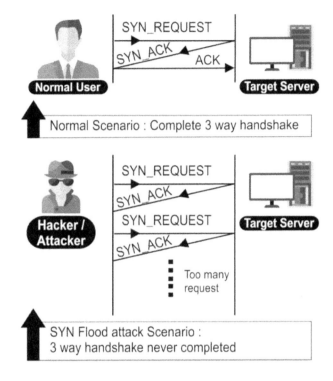

The three-way handshake

1. First, a "synchronize", or **SYN** message, is sent to the host machine to start the conversation.

2. Next, the request is "acknowledged" by the server. It sends an **ACK** flag to the machine that started the "handshake" process and awaits for the connection to be closed.

3. The connection is completed when the requesting machine closes the connection.

This process continues until all open ports are saturated with requests and none are available for legitimate users to connect to.

Ping of Death attack

A **ping of death** (**POD**) attack is performed by manipulating the IP protocol by sending packets larger than the maximum byte allowance, which under IPv4 is 65,535 bytes. Large packets are divided across multiple IP packets called fragments, and once reassembled, create a packet larger than 65,535 bytes. The resulting large packet causes servers to crash or become inaccessible.

Reflected attack

A reflected attack is performed by creating forged packets that will be sent out to as many computers as possible. When these computers receive the packets, they will reply, but the reply will be a spoofed address that actually routes to the target. All of the computers will attempt to communicate at once, and this will cause the site to be flooded with requests until the server resources are exhausted.

NTP amplification

An **NTP** (**Network Time Protocol**) amplification attack is performed by spoofing a victim's NTP infrastructure and use Open NTP servers that sends small requests resulting in a very high volume of NTP responses.

Peer-to-peer attacks

A peer-to-peer server attack is performed by exploiting the route traffic to the target website. When done successfully, people using the file-sharing hub are instead sent to the target website until the website is routed and sent offline.

CHAPTER 15

Wireless Network Hacking

Wireless Network

Wireless networks are computer networks that are not connected by cables of any kind. It use radio waves to connect devices, such as laptops to the Internet, the business network and applications. When laptops are connected to Wi-Fi hotspots in public places, the connection is established to that business's wireless network.

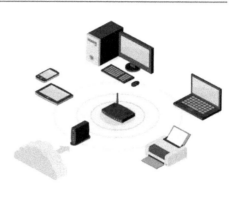

 NOTE In an *Ethernet network,* the data is carried in frames on copper or fiber-optic cabling, whereas in a *Wi-Fi network,* the data travels across open air.

Wireless network types

Type	Coverage	Performance	Standards	Applications
Wireless PAN	Within reach of a person	Moderate	Wireless PAN within reach of a person, moderate Bluetooth, IEEE 802.15, and IrDa cable replacement for peripherals	Cable replacement for peripherals

Wireless LAN	Within a building or campus	High	IEEE 802.11, Wi-Fi, and HiperLAN	Mobile extension of wired networks
Wireless MAN	Within a city	High	Proprietary, IEEE 802.16, and WIMAX	Fixed wireless between homes and businesses and the Internet
Wireless WAN	Worldwide	Low	CDPD and cellular 2G, 2.5G, and 3G	Mobile access to the Internet from outdoor areas
PAN: Personal area network; **LAN:** Local area network; **MAN:** Metropolitan area network; **WAN:** Wide area network				

Radio frequency transmission factors

Radio frequencies (RFs) are generated by antennas that propagate the waves into the air.

Antennas fall under two different categories: **directional** and **omni-directional**.

Directional antennas are commonly used in point-to-point configurations (connecting two distant buildings), and sometimes point-to-multipoint (connecting two WLANs). An example of a directional antenna is a Yagi antenna: this antenna allows you to adjust the direction and focus of the signal to intensify your range/reach.

Omni-directional antennas are used in point-to-multipoint configurations, where they distribute the wireless signal to other computers or devices in your WLAN. An access point would use an omni-directional antenna. These antennas can also be used for point-to-point connections, but they lack the distance that directional antennas supply.

Three main factors influencing signal distortion

- **Absorption objects**: They absorb the RF waves, such as walls, ceilings, and floors
- **Scattering objects**: These disperse the RF waves, such as rough plaster on a wall, carpet on the floor, or drop-down ceiling tiles

- **Reflection objects**: These reflect the RF waves, such as metal and glass**Responsible body**

The **International Telecommunication Union-Radio Communication Sector** (**ITU-R**) is responsible for managing the RF spectrum and satellite orbits for wireless communications; its main purpose is to provide for cooperation and coexistence of standards and implementations across country boundaries. Two standards bodies are primarily responsible for implementing WLANs:

- *IEEE* defines the mechanical process of how WLANs are implemented in the 802.11 standards so that vendors can create compatible products.

- *Wi-Fi Alliance* basically certifies companies by ensuring that their products follow the 802.11 standards, thus allowing customers to buy WLAN products from different vendors without having to be concerned about any compatibility issues.

Transmission method

Direct sequence spread spectrum (**DSSS**): DSSS uses one channel to send data across all frequencies within that channel. **Complementary Code Keying** (**CCK**) is a method for encoding transmissions for higher data rates, such as 5.5 and 11 Mbps, but it still allows backward compatibility with the original 802.11 standard, which supports only 1 and 2 Mbps speeds. 802.11b and 802.11g support this transmission method.

OFDM (**orthogonal frequency division multiplexing**): OFDM increases data rates by using a spread spectrum: modulation. 802.11a and 802.11g support this transmission method.

MIMO (**multiple input multiple output**) **transmission**: This uses DSSS and/or OFDM by spreading its signal across 14 overlapping channels at 5 MHz intervals. 802.11n uses this. Use of 802.11n requires multiple antennas.

WLAN standards

Standards	802.11a	802.11b	802.11g	802.11n
Data rate	54 Mbps	11 Mbps	54 Mbps	248 Mbps (with 2 × 2 antennas)
Throughput	23 Mbps	4.3 Mbps	19 Mbps	74 Mbps
Frequency	5 GHz	2.4 GHz	2.4 GHz	2.4 and/or 5 GHz
Compatibility	None	With 802.11g and the original 802.11	With 802.11b	802.11a, b, and g
Range (meters)	35–120	38–140	38–140	70–250
Number of channels	3	Up to 23	3	14
Transmission	OFDM	DSSS	D S S S / OFDM	MIMO

Wireless network security

Wireless network security is the process of designing, implementing, and ensuring security on a wireless computer network. It can protect a wireless network from unauthorized and malicious access attempts. Wireless network security is also known as *Wireless Security Protocol*. Some of the common encryption standards to ensure wireless network security are **Wired Equivalent Policy** (**WEP**) and **Wi-Fi Protected Access** (**WPA**).

WEP

WEP can provide the same level of security as wired networks. It is also called as *Wireless Encryption Protocol*. WEP is part of the IEEE 802.11 wireless networking standard and was designed to provide the same level of security as that of a wired LAN. However, WEP has many well-known security flaws, is difficult to configure, and is easily broken. In WEP, the router and the wireless stations must be configured with the same WEP key.

WPA

WPA aims to provide stronger wireless data encryption than WEP, but not everyone has or was able to jump onboard with the new wireless encryption technology. In order to use WPA, all devices on the network must be configured for WPA. Most current WPA implementations use a **pre-shared key** (**PSK**), commonly referred to as WPA Personal, and the **Temporal Key Integrity Protocol** (**TKIP**, pronounced tee-kip) for encryption. WPA Enterprise uses an authentication server to generate keys or certificates. WPA included a new feature called **WPS** (**Wi-Fi Protected Setup**), which was supposed to make it easier for users to connect devices to the wireless router. However, it ended up having vulnerabilities that allowed security researchers to crack a WPA key within a short period of time also.

WPA version 2

WPA version 2 (**WPA2**) is an 802.11i wireless security standard-based protocol. The most important improvement of WPA2 over WPA was the usage of the **Advanced Encryption Standard** (**AES**) for encryption. WPA2 is the most secure protocol, and AES with **Cipher Block Chaining Message Authentication Code Protocol** (**CCMP**) is the most secure encryption. In addition, WPS should be disabled as it's very easy to hack and capture the router PIN, which can then be used to connect to the router.

Wireless network hacking

Wireless network hacking deals with the hacking and cracking of wireless network system. Some major hacking techniques of wireless network are described as follows.

- **Sniffing**: This involves intercepting packets as they are transmitted over a network. It involves capturing passwords or other confidential information from an unencrypted WLAN or hotspot.

- **Man-in-the-middle** (**MITM**) **attack**: This involves eavesdropping on a network and capturing sensitive information.

- **Denial-of-service attack**: This is intended to deny legitimate users network resources. It can be performed at the **Logical Link Control** (**LLC**) layer by generating deauthentication frames (deauth attacks), by continuously generating bogus frames, or by having a wireless NIC send a constant stream of raw RF (Queensland attack).

- **WEP cracking**: This is the process of exploiting security weaknesses in wireless networks and gaining unauthorized access. It refers to exploits on networks that use WEP to implement security controls. There are mainly two types of WEP cracking, namely, *passive cracking* and *active cracking*. *Passive cracking* has no effect on the network traffic until the WEP security has been cracked. It is difficult to detect. *Active cracking* has an increased load effect on the network traffic. It is easy to detect compared to passive cracking. It is more effective than passive cracking.

- **WPA cracking**: This involves in a 256 PSK or passphrase for authentications of WPA. Short passphrases are vulnerable to dictionary attacks and other attacks that can be used to crack passwords.

- **MAC spoofing**: This can be performed by the hacker pretending to be a legitimate WLAN client and bypasses MAC filters by spoofing another user's MAC address. WIDSs can detect MAC spoofing, and not using MAC filtering is a way to avoid MAC spoofing attacks.

Wireless network hacking and cracking tools

Tool	Description	Download website
Aircrack	Network sniffer, WEP and WAP cracker	*www.aircrack-ng.org*
AirSnort	Wireless LAN password cracker	*www.sourceforge.net/ projects/airsnort*
Airjack	Wi-Fi 802.11 packet injection tool (DoS attack and MITM attack)	*www.sourceforge.net/ projects/airjack*
CoWPAtty	Wireless password cracker	*www.sourceforge.net/ projects/cowpatty*
Kismet	Wi-Fi 802.11 a/b/g/n layer two wireless network sniffer and intrusion detection system	*www.kismetwireless.net*
Cain and Abel	Sniffer and wireless network passwords cracker	*www.oxid.it/cain.html*
Wireshark	Network protocol analyzer	*www.wireshark.org*

Cracking wireless password using Cain and Abel (in Windows)

1. Open the **Cain and Abel** tool (Run as administrator).

2. Click on **Wireless Passwords** on the left panel:

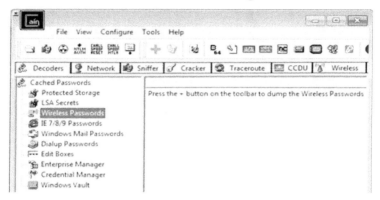

3. Now click on the **Add to list** (+ button):

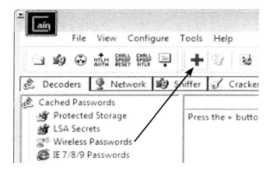

4. Now, you can see the Wi-Fi adapters along with password, as the following screenshot:

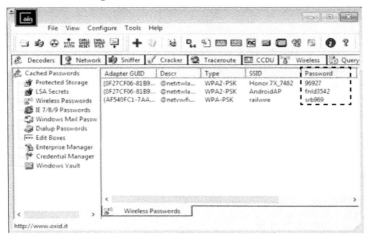

Cracking a Wi-Fi password (in Kali Linux)

Open the **Terminal** and find out the name of your wireless adapter by entering *ifconfig* in the Terminal. Wireless adapter is set to default name as **wlan0**.

1. Type *airmon-ng check kill* and press *Enter*.

2. Enable the monitor mode. Now, we use the tool called **airmon-ng** to create a virtual interface. Type *airmon-ng start wlan0* and press *Enter*.

3. Start capturing packets by typing **airodump-ng wlan0mon** and press **Enter**. Then, press Ctrl + C.

4. Type *reaver -i wlan0mon -b (BSSID) -vv -K 1* and press *Enter*. In BSSID, you can copy and paste the BSSID of the victim; for example: *reaver -i wlan0mon -b B0:C5:55:89:5E:60 -vv -K 1*

5. You can see the password in the **WPA PSK** field.

CHAPTER 16

Web Server and Application Vulnerabilities

Web server

A web server is a computer system where the web content is stored. Generally, it is used to host the websites. A web server can also be referred to as the hardware, the computer, or the software, and is the computer application that helps to deliver content that can be accessed

through the Internet. The primary function of a web server is to deliver web pages on the request to clients using the **Hypertext Transfer Protocol** (**HTTP**).

Web server working

A web server responds to the client request in either of the following two ways:

- Sending the file to the client associated with the requested URL.

- Generating a response by invoking a script and communicating with database.

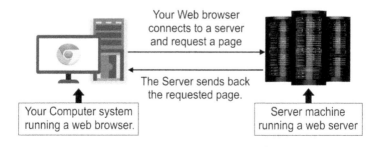

Your Web browser connects to a server and request a page

The Server sends back the requested page.

Your Computer system running a web browser.

Server machine running a web server

Types of web servers

There are basically four primary web servers: (i) *Apache* (provided by Apache), (ii) **IIS** (**Internet Information Services**) (provided by Microsoft), (iii) *nginx* (provided by NGINX, Inc. and pronounced as "Engine X"), and (iv) **GWS** (provided by Google and short for **Google web server**).

File servers

File servers are often responsible for the availability of stored files and their management, as well as security. You can send and receive files at the user's request. These are not like sharing servers; they are more like the filing cabinets of the Internet world. File servers are often categorized by how the files on the server are accessed. Different methods of a file server are as follows:

- **Internet file servers: FTP** (**File Transfer Protocol**) and HTTP

- **LAN file servers:** SMB/CIFS Protocol and NFS Protocol

File servers are different from web servers because they do not provide dynamic web content like web servers. Instead they only provide static files.

Application servers

An application server is a server that is dedicated to serving a certain piece of software. It is often used in conjunction with other servers and software. For example, you may sign up for online gaming and be directed to servers set up solely for the gaming software. The advantages of an application server are data and code integrity, centralized configuration, security, performance, lower cost of ownership, and transaction support.

Types of application servers are as follows:

- Java application servers
- .Net Framework
- PHP application servers
- Open source application servers
- Mobile application servers

Inter-server-level devices

Inter-server-level devices bypass servers in order to send signals directly from one place to another in an organized fashion, such as how a person is able to download one file from multiple computers at one time.

Message servers

Message servers allow things such as real-time communication between users. They may include IRC servers, chat servers, and groupware. The methods of communication are fairly flexible.

Proxy servers

A proxy server act as a mediator between server-to-filter requests made by users and a client program. It allows the management of e-mails and shared connections.

There are two types of proxy servers: *open proxies* and *reverse proxies*.

Open proxies forward a proxy server that is accessible to any user. Anonymous open proxies allow the users to access them to conceal their IP address while using the Internet. The level of anonymity varies, and these often aren't entirely secretive as their methods, which will cause the client to real itself.

Reverse proxies are a type of server that appears to be an ordinary server. A user who requests information from the server will have their request forwarded to one or more proxy servers that allow the user to receive their request as if it were from the original server all while having no information as to the original server.

Proxy server uses

Proxy servers have a wide range of uses, including both malicious and legitimate uses. For example, large corporations may use proxy servers to protect their data while someone may avoid government, business, or school censorship with the use of a proxy.

Database servers

Database servers can manage a database, as it is stored on the server. They may use the SQL database management system. The server can search through information and send any requested information back to the client.

Mail servers

As the name suggests, a mail server is the sort of server you can use to control an e-mail. A server may be set up with the expressed idea of it controlling and handling e-mails only. It sends, receives, and stores your e-mails.

There are two primary types of mail servers: **IMAP** and **POP3** servers. IMAP is quickly becoming the most popular server as it allows you to read your mail on multiple devices. Most people will not need to (nor want to) run their own mail server, as Google, Microsoft, and plenty of other corporations offer free e-mail.

Web server attacks

Some common web server attacks are as follows:

Attack	Description
Directory traversal attacks	It exploits bugs in the web server to gain unauthorized access to files and folders that are not in the public domain. After exploitation, the attacker can download sensitive information, execute commands on the server, or install malicious software.
Denial-of-service Attacks	In this attack, the web server may crash or become unavailable to the legitimate users.
Domain Name System hijacking	In this attack, the DNS setting are changed to point to the attacker's web server. All traffic that was supposed to be sent to the web server is redirected to another (wrong) server.
Sniffing	In this attack, unencrypted data sent over the network may be intercepted and used to gain unauthorized access to the web server.
Phishing	In this attack, the attacker impersonates the websites and directs traffic to the fake website. Unsuspecting users may be tricked into submitting sensitive data such as login details, credit card numbers, and so on.
Pharming	In this attack, the attacker compromises the **Domain Name System** (**DNS**) servers or on the user computer so that traffic is directed to a malicious site.
Defacement	In this attack, the attacker replaces the organization's website with a different page that contains the hacker's name, images, and may include background music and messages.

Web server attack tools

Tool	Description	Download website
Metasploit	It is used for developing, testing, discovering vulnerabilities in web servers and writing exploits that can be used to compromise the server.	*www.metasploit. com*
MPack	It is a web exploitation tool written in PHP and is backed by MySQL as the database engine. It can redirected to malicious download websites, after it exploits the server.	*www.sourceforge. net/projects/mpack-win*
Zeus	It is used to turn a computer system into a bot or zombie to perform a denial-of-service attack or sending spam mails.	*www.github.com/ Visgean/Zeus*

Web application

A web application (website) is an application based on the client–server model. The server provides the database access and the business logic. It is hosted on a web server. The client application runs on the client web browser. Web applications are usually written in languages such as Java, C#, and VB.Net, PHP, and HTML. The database engines used in web applications include MySQL, MS SQL Server, PostgreSQL, SQLite, etc.

Web application vulnerabilities

Major web application vulnerabilities are as follows.

Cross-site scripting

Cross-site scripting (**XSS**) is a code injection attack that allows an attacker to execute malicious script in another user's web browser. These attacks can be carried out using HTML, JavaScript, VBScript, ActiveX, Flash, etc. The attacker exploits a vulnerability in a website that the victim visits, in order to get the website to deliver the malicious script. To the victim's browser, the malicious script appears to be a legitimate part of the website, and the website has, thus, acted as an unintentional accomplice to the attacker.

SQL injection

A **structured query language** (**SQL**) injection uses malicious SQL code for backend database manipulation to access information that was not intended to be displayed. This information may include any number of items, including sensitive company data, user lists, or private customer details. This type of attack may result in the unauthorized viewing of user lists, the deletion of entire tables, and in certain cases, the attacker gaining administrative rights to a database, all of which are highly detrimental to a business.

Example of an SQL injection vulnerability

Firstly, understand how server-side scripting languages handle SQL queries. For example, let's say functionality in the web application generates a string with the following SQL statement:

$statement = "SELECT * FROM users WHERE username = 'som' AND password = 'mysecretpw'";

This SQL statement is passed to a function that sends the string to the connected database where it is parsed, executed, and returns a result.

As you might have noticed, the statement contains some new, special characters:

- *** (asterisk)** is an instruction for the SQL database to return all columns for the selected database row.
- **= (equals)** is an instruction for the SQL database to only return values that match the searched string.
- **' (single quote mark)** is used to tell the SQL database where the search string starts or ends.

Now, consider the following example in which a website user is able to change the values of **'$user'** and **'$password'**, such as in a login form:

$statement = "SELECT * FROM users WHERE username = '$user' AND password
= '$password'";

An attacker can easily insert any special SQL syntax inside the statement, if the input is not sanitized by the application:

$statement = "SELECT * FROM users WHERE username = 'admin'; -- ' AND password = 'anything'"; = 'anything'";

From the preceding, [**admin'; --**] is the attacker's input, which contains two new, special characters:

; **(semicolon)** is used to instruct the SQL parser that the current statement has ended. **-- (double hyphen)** instructs the SQL parser that the rest of the line is a comment and should not be executed.

This SQL injection effectively removes the password verification and returns a dataset for an existing user—**'admin'** in this case. The attacker can now log in with an administrator account, without having to specify a password.

 Some major SQL injection tools are BSQL Hacker, SQLmap, SQLninja, Safe3 SQL Injector, SQLSus, Mole, etc.

Denial-of -service attacks (DoS)

For more details, please refer to *Chapter 14, Denial-of-Service (DoS) Attacks*.

Cross-site request forgery

Cross-site request forgery occurs when a malicious website, e-mail, or program causes a user's browser to perform an unwanted action on a trusted site for which the user is currently authenticated. This attack can use logged-on victim's browser to send a forged HTTP request, including the victim's session cookie and any other automatically included authentication information to a vulnerable web application. A link will be sent by the attacker to the victim; when the user clicks on the URL when logged into the original website, the data will be stolen from the website.

Arbitrary code execution

Malicious code that utilizes system calls and user input could allow an attacker to run an arbitrary command on the filesystem. This attack bears many resemblances to an SQL injection, in that the attacker manipulates input to cause execution of unintended commands.

 Some major web application security scanners are Burp Suite, Netsparker, Arachni, W3af, Vega, etc.

CHAPTER 17

Penetration Testing

Penetration testing (pen test)

Penetration testing is an authorized simulated attack on a computer system performed to identify the vulnerabilities and evaluate the risk of the system. Penetration testing is conducted by professional ethical hackers who mainly use commercial, open source tools, automated tools, and manual checks. There are no restrictions; the most important objective here is to uncover as many security flaws as possible.

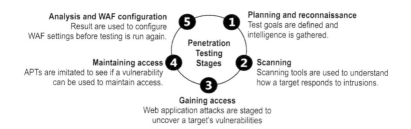

Analysis and WAF configuration 5 — Result are used to configure WAF settings before testing is run again.

Planning and reconnaissance 1 — Test goals are defined and intelligence is gathered.

Penetration Testing Stages

Maintaining access 4 — APTs are imitated to see if a vulnerability can be used to maintain access.

Scanning 2 — Scanning tools are used to understand how a target responds to intrusions.

Gaining access 3 — Web application attacks are staged to uncover a target's vulnerabilities

Types of penetration tests

Basically, the penetration tests are classified into five different types. These are as follows:

- Network service tests
- Web application tests
- Client-side tests
- Wireless network tests
- Social engineering tests

Network service tests

The network service tests type of pen test aims to discover vulnerabilities and gaps in the network infrastructure of the clients. As the network can have both internal and external access points, it is mandatory to run tests locally at the client site and remotely from the outer world. The testers should target the following network areas in their penetration tests:Firewall config testing

- Stateful analysis testing
- Firewall bypass testing
- IPS deception
- DNS-level attacks that include *zone transfer testing, switching or routing-based testing, and any miscellaneous network parameter testing*

Also, there are a set of software modules that the penetration test should cover; these are SSH client/server tests, network databases such as MYSQL/SQL Server, exchange or SMTP mail servers, and FTP client/server tests.

Web application tests

Web applications, browsers, and their components such as ActiveX, applets, plug-ins, scriptlets fall in the scope of this type of pen testing. As this test examines the end points of each web apps that a user might have to interact on a regular basis, it needs thorough planning and time investment. Also, with the increase in threats coming from the web applications, the ways to test them are continuously evolving.

Client-side tests

The goal of client-side tests is to pinpoint security threats that emerge locally. For example, there could be a flaw in a software application running on the user's workstation that a hacker can easily exploit. These may be programs or applications such as PuTTy, Git clients, sniffers, browsers (Chrome, Firefox, Safari, IE, Opera), and even presentation, as well as content creation packages such as MS Power Point, Adobe Page Maker, Photoshop, and media players.

Wireless network tests

A wireless network test intends to analyze the wireless devices deployed on the client site. The list of devices include items like tablets, laptops, notebooks, iPods, smartphones, etc. Apart from the gadgets, the penetration tester should consider preparing tests for the following:

- Protocols used for configuring wireless helps find out the weak areas.

- Access points for wireless setup enables in identifying the ones violating the access rights.

Usually, these type of tests should take place at the customer end. The hardware used to run pen tests needs to be connected to the wireless system for exposing a vulnerability.

Social engineering tests

The social engineering type of test also runs as an important part of penetration testing. It paves ways for verifying the "Human Network" of an organization. This pen test imitates attacks that the employees of a company could attempt to initiate a breach. However, it can further split up into two sub-categories.

- **Remote tests**: These intend to trick an engineer (employee) to compromise confidential data using electronic means. The tester could conduct such an attack via a phishing e-mail campaign.

- **Physical tests**: These require a direct contact with the subject to retrieve the sensitive information. It might involve human handling tactics such as dumpster diving, imitation, and intimidation or convince the subject via phone calls.

CHAPTER 18

Surface Web, Deep Web, and Dark Net

Surface Web

The surface Web consists of all Web-based content that can be found in search engines. It can be described as the common or regular Internet, which is used by many users to read blogs/ news, visit social networking sites, and shopping sites. The websites, webpages, and information that you find using Web search engines, such as Google, Yahoo, Bing, only show that you are exploring just the surface of the Web. Some major surface web browsers are Google Chrome, Mozilla Firefox, Opera, Safari, Microsoft Edge, etc.

The easy view to understand the surface Web:Accessible (to general public)

- Indexed for search engines
- Little illegal activity
- Relatively small in size

Deep Web

The deep Web is the Web that exists in places that cannot be accessed by search engines, but can be accessed if you have an address. It contains databases, dynamic content, some forums, sites that have never been indexed, and any other content that Google and company have neither listed nor indexed. Generally, the content that you cannot find using the search engine is termed as deep Web. Tor browser is the well-known deep Web browser.

Easy views to understand the deep Web:

- Accessible by password, encryption, or through gateway software
- Not indexed for search engines
- Less illegal activity than the dark Web
- Huge in size and growing exponentially

Surface Web versus deep Web

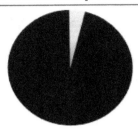

— **Surface Web**   ■ **Deep Web**

Dark Web

The dark Web (or Darknet) is only a subset of the deep Web. It is not only not indexed, but that also requires something special to be able to access it, for example, specific anonymizing (proxy) software or authentication to gain access. The Darknet often sits on top of additional sub-networks, such as Tor, I2P, and Freenet, and is often associated with criminal activities, including buying and selling drugs, pornography, gambling. The most common software used to access the dark Web is **the Onion Router** (**Tor**) browser.

The easy view to understand the dark Web (or Darknet):

- Restricted to special browsers
- Not indexed for search engines
- Large scale illegal activity
- Unmeasurable due to nature

Deep Web versus dark Web

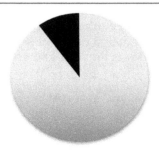

— **Deep Web**   ■ **Dark Web**

Overview of surface, deep, and dark Web

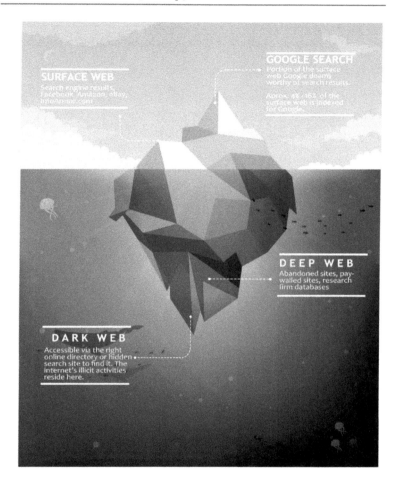

Tor

The Tor browser helps a user to access the deep Web and dark Web, like numerous hidden websites and services which cannot be accessed on the regular Internet. It can also be used to visit everyday Internet websites. Tor powers them using its protocol known as **Tor hidden service protocol**.

NOTE The websites limited to the Tor network have a special *.onion* address. Due to this, Tor's Darknet is also known as *onionland*.

Visit the *www.torproject.org* website to download the Tor browser.

The following things are accessible by the Tor browser:

- Government documents/information
- Political documents/information
- WikiLeaks information
- Online black market
- Cryptocurrency (bitcoin) mining
- Illegal adult content

www.torproject.org

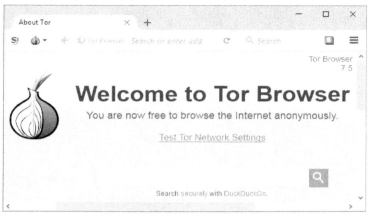

Tor Browser